NORTH SEA

collection eight

CONTENTS

NORTH SEA

... is inspired by the traditional fisherman knit and is a celebration of nautical cables and Celtic twists, complimented by Nordic inspired Fair Isle. The modern and classic fit garments are perfect to wear at home or for walking on a windswept beach. The colour palette is neutral using the quintessential blue and grey tones synonymous with seascapes of the North Sea. The collection was photographed on the remote and beautiful island of Unst, the most northerly of the Shetland Islands...a perfect location to experience the wildness of where the North Sea meets the North Atlantic Ocean.

Marie X

Bute

Bute

Islay

Islay

Soay

Soay

Skye

Eriskay

Eriskay

Tiree

Uist

Uist

GALLERY

BUTE
Main image pages 6, 8, 9, 10 & 11
Pattern page 50

ISLAY
Main image pages 12, 13, 14 & 15
Pattern page 68

SOAY
Main image pages 16, 17, 18, 19 & 74
Pattern page 46

SKYE
Main image pages 20 & 21
Pattern page 56

ERISKAY
Main image pages 22, 23, 24 & 25
Pattern page 43

TIREE
Main image pages 26, 27, 28, 29 & 39
Pattern page 60

ARRAN
Main image pages 30, 31, 32 & 33
Pattern page 40

UIST
Main image pages 34, 35, 36 & 37
Pattern page 64

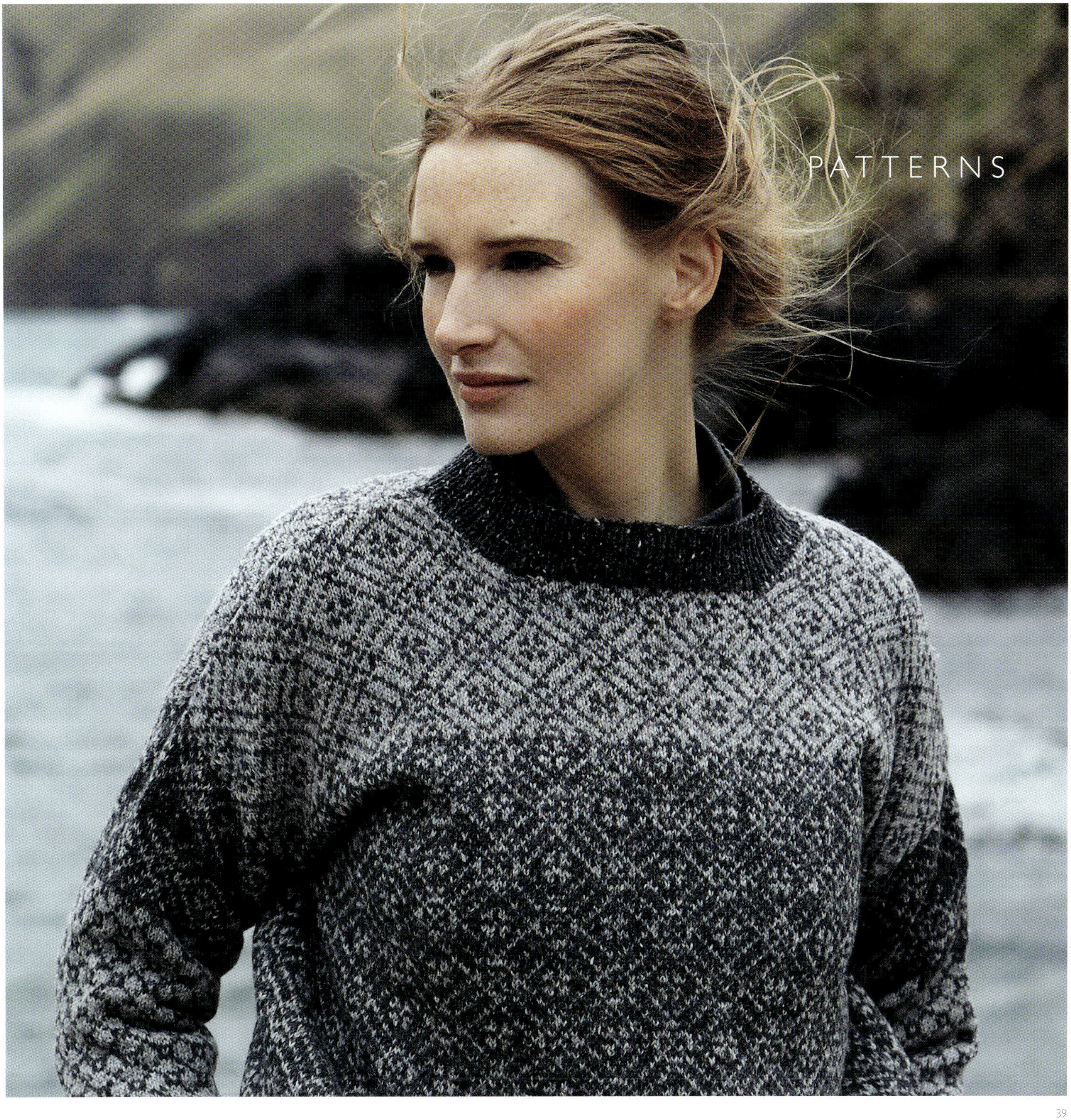
PATTERNS

ARRAN

● ● ●

	S	M	L	XL	XXL	
To fit bust	81-86	91-97	102-107	112-117	122-127	cm
	32-34	36-38	40-42	44-46	48-50	in

Rowan Felted Tweed

	10	10	11	12	14	x 50gm

(photographed in Granite 191)

Needles

1 pair 2¾mm (no 12) (US 2) needles
1 pair 3¼mm (no 10) (US 3) needles
2¾mm (no 12) (US 2) circular needle
3¼mm (no 10) (US 3) circular needle

Tension

31 sts and 34½ rows to 10 cm measured over patt using 3¼mm (US 3) needles.

SPECIAL ABBREVIATIONS

Tw2L = K into back of second st on left needle, K tog tbl first 2 sts on left needle and slip both sts off left needle together; **Tw2R** = K2tog leaving sts on left needle, K first st again and slip both sts off left needle together.

KEY

□ K on RS, P on WS   • P on RS, K on WS   ⧅ Tw2L   ⧄ Tw2R

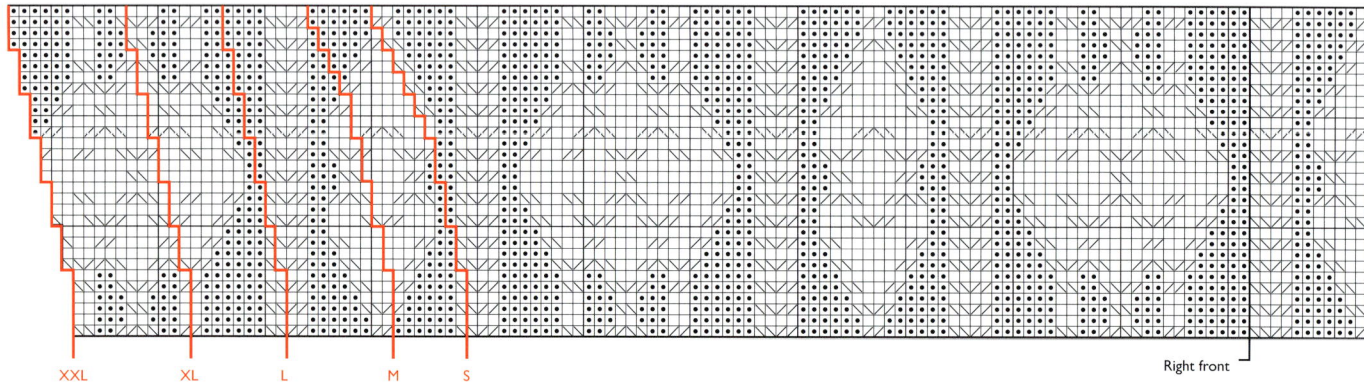

XXL   XL   L   M   S

Right front

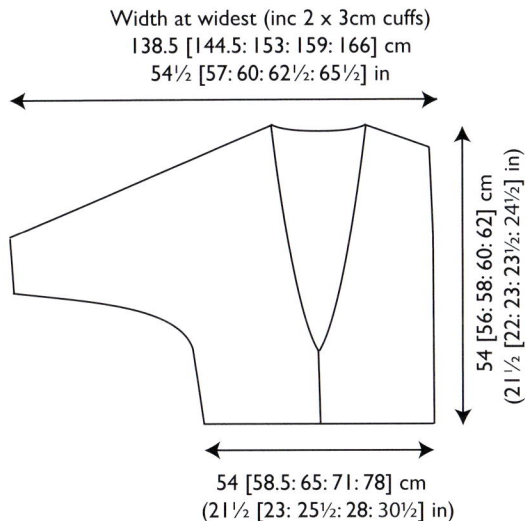

Width at widest (inc 2 x 3cm cuffs)
138.5 [144.5: 153: 159: 166] cm
54½ [57: 60: 62½: 65½] in

54 [56: 58: 60: 62] cm
(21½ [22: 23: 23½: 24½] in)

54 [58.5: 65: 71: 78] cm
(21½ [23: 25½: 28: 30½] in)

BACK
Using 2¾mm (US 2) needles cast on 167 [181: 201: 219: 241] sts.
Row 1 (RS): K1, *P1, K1, rep from * to end.
Row 2: As row 1.
These 2 rows form moss st.

Work in moss st for a further 38 rows, inc 1 st at end of last row and ending with RS facing for next row. 168 [182: 202: 220: 242] sts.
Change to 3¼mm (US 3) needles.
Beg and ending rows as indicated and repeating the 30 row patt repeat throughout, cont in patt from chart as folls:
Work 6 rows, ending with RS facing for next row.
Inc 1 st at each end of next and 3 [4: 6: 7: 9] foll 4th rows, then on foll 10 [9: 7: 8: 6] alt rows, then on foll 17 [17: 17: 15: 15] rows, taking inc sts into patt and ending with RS facing for next row.
230 [244: 264: 282: 304] sts. (**Note:** As the number of sts increases and there become too many to comfortably fit on straight needles, change to circular needle.)
Taking all cast-on sts into patt, cast on 12 [11: 10: 9: 8] sts at beg of next 2 [6: 6: 8: 6] rows, then 13 [12: 11: 10: 9] sts at beg of foll 12 [10: 12: 12: 16] rows. 410 [430: 456: 474: 496] sts.
Work 34 [36: 38: 38: 40] rows, ending with RS facing for next row.
Shape overarm and shoulders
Keeping patt correct, cast off 6 [6: 6: 7: 7] sts at beg of next 50 [30: 6: 46: 26] rows, then – [7: 7: 8: 8] sts at beg of foll – [20: 44: 4: 24] rows.
110 [110: 112: 120: 122] sts.
Shape back neck
Next row (RS): Cast off 7 [7: 7: 8: 8] sts, patt until there are 25 [25: 25:

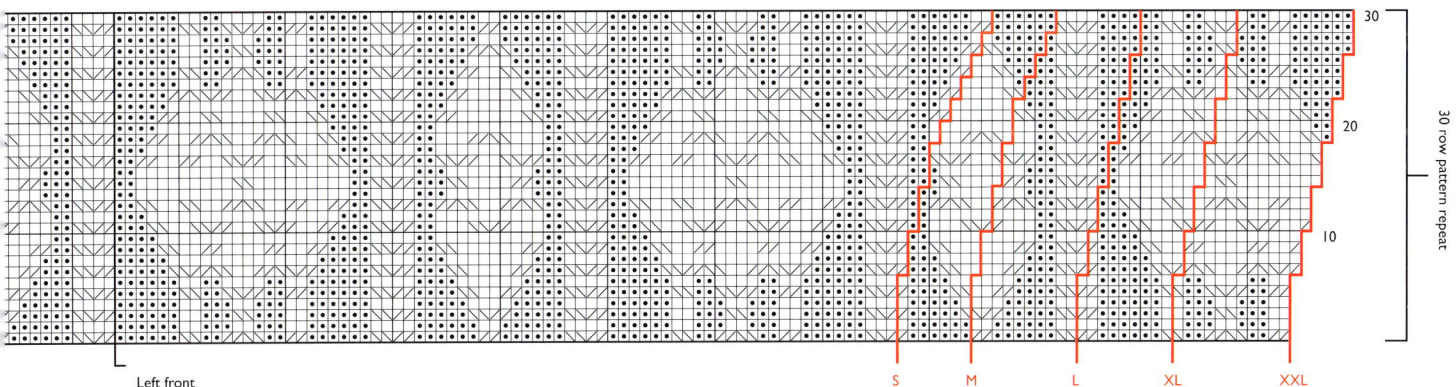

Left front

S   M   L   XL   XXL

30 row pattern repeat

30

20

10

28: 28] sts on right needle and turn, leaving rem sts on a holder.
Work each side of neck separately.
Dec 1 st at neck edge of next 4 rows **and at same time** cast off
7 [7: 7: 8: 8] sts at beg of 2nd and foll alt row.
Work 1 row.
Cast off rem 7 [7: 7: 8: 8] sts.
With RS facing, slip centre 46 [46: 48: 48: 50] sts onto a holder, rejoin yarn
and patt to end.
Complete to match first side, reversing shapings.

LEFT FRONT
Using 2¾mm (US 2) needles cast on 73 [79: 89: 99: 109] sts.
Work in moss st as given for back for 40 rows, inc 0 [1: 1: 0: 1] st at end
of last row and ending with RS facing for next row. 73 [80: 90: 99: 110] sts.
Change to 3¼mm (US 3) needles.
Beg and ending rows as indicated, cont in patt from chart as folls:
Work 6 rows, ending with RS facing for next row.
Inc 1 st at beg of next and 3 [4: 6: 7: 9] foll 4th rows, then on foll
10 [9: 7: 8: 6] alt rows, then at same edge on foll 17 [17: 17: 15: 15] rows,
taking inc sts into patt and ending with RS facing for next row.
104 [111: 121: 130: 141] sts.
Taking all cast-on sts into patt, cast on 12 [11: 10: 9: 8] sts at beg of next
and foll 0 [2: 2: 3: 2] alt rows, then 13 [12: 11: 10: 9] sts at beg of foll
2 [2: 2: 3: 4] alt rows. 142 [168: 173: 196: 201] sts.
Work 1 row, ending with RS facing for next row.
Shape front slope
Keeping patt correct, cast on 13 [12: 11: 10: 9] sts at beg of next and foll
3 [2: 3: 2: 3] alt rows **and at same time** dec 1 st at end (front slope edge)
of next and foll 6th [-: 6th: 4th: 4th] row. 192 [203: 215: 224: 235] sts.
Dec 1 st at front slope edge on 6th [2nd: 6th: 6th: 2nd] and 4 [5: 5: 5: 6]
foll 6th rows. 187 [197: 209: 218: 228] sts.
Work 5 [5: 3: 3: 3] rows, ending with RS facing for next row.
Shape overarm and shoulder
Keeping patt correct, cast off 6 [6: 6: 7: 7] sts at beg of next and foll
24 [14: 2: 22: 12] alt rows, then 7 [7: 7: 8: 8] sts at beg of foll
3 [13: 25: 5: 15] alt rows **and at same time** dec 1 st at front slope edge of
next [next: 3rd: 3rd: 3rd] and 7 [7: 8: 8: 8] foll 6th rows, then on
1 [1: 0: 0: 0] foll 8th row.
Work 1 row.

Cast off rem 7 [7: 7: 8: 8] sts.

RIGHT FRONT
Using 2¾mm (US 2) needles cast on 73 [79: 89: 99: 109] sts.
Work in moss st as given for back for 40 rows, inc 0 [1: 1: 0: 1] st at beg
of last row and ending with RS facing for next row. 73 [80: 90: 99: 110] sts.
Change to 3¼mm (US 3) needles.
Beg and ending rows as indicated, cont in patt from chart as folls:
Work 6 rows, ending with RS facing for next row.
Inc 1 st at end of next and 3 [4: 6: 7: 9] foll 4th rows, then on foll
10 [9: 7: 8: 6] alt rows, then at same edge on foll 17 [17: 17: 15: 15] rows,
taking inc sts into patt and ending with RS facing for next row.
104 [111: 121: 130: 141] sts.
Complete to match left front, reversing shapings.

MAKING UP
Press as described on the information page.
Join both overarm and shoulders seam using back stitch, or mattress
stitch if preferred.
Front band
With RS facing and using 2¾mm (US 2) circular needle, beg and ending
at front cast-on edges, pick up and knit 81 [87: 90: 96: 99] sts up right
front opening edge to beg of front slope shaping, 96 [96: 99: 99: 103] sts
up right front slope, and 5 sts down right side of back neck, K across
46 [46: 48: 48: 50] sts on back holder inc 1 st at centre, then pick up and
knit 5 sts up left side of back neck, 96 [96: 99: 99: 103] sts down left front
slope to beg of front slope shaping, and 81 [87: 90: 96: 99] sts down left
front opening edge. 411 [423: 437: 449: 465] sts.
Work in moss st as given for back until front band measures 5 cm from
pick up, ending with RS facing for next row.
Cast off in moss st.
Cuffs (both alike)
With RS facing and using 2¾mm (US 2) circular needle, pick up and
knit 61 [65: 67: 67: 71] sts evenly along straight row-end edge of sleeve
extension.
Work in moss st as given for back until cuff measures 3 cm from pick up,
ending with RS facing for next row.
Cast off in moss st.
Join side and sleeve seams.

sts off left needle together; **Tw2R** = K2tog leaving sts on left needle, K first st again and slip both sts off left needle together.

BACK

Using 2¼mm (US 1) needles cast on 186 [204: 226: 248: 274] sts.
Beg and ending rows as indicated, cont in patt from chart for body as folls:
Work chart rows 1 to 4, 7 times, ending with RS facing for next row.
Change to 3mm (US 2/3) needles.
Now repeating chart rows 5 to 40 **throughout**, cont as folls:
Dec 1 st at each end of 13th and 3 foll 24th rows.
178 [196: 218: 240: 266] sts.
Cont straight until back meas 36 [37: 38: 39: 40] cm, ending with RS facing for next row.

Shape armholes

Keeping patt correct, cast off 9 [11: 13: 15: 17] sts at beg of next 2 rows.
160 [174: 192: 210: 232] sts.
Dec 1 st at each end of next 9 [11: 13: 15: 17] rows, then on foll 8 [9: 11: 12: 15] alt rows. 126 [134: 144: 156: 168] sts.
Cont straight until armhole meas 17 [18: 19: 20: 21] cm, ending with RS facing for next row.

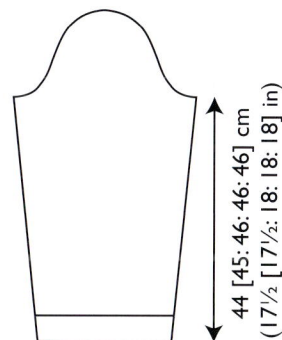

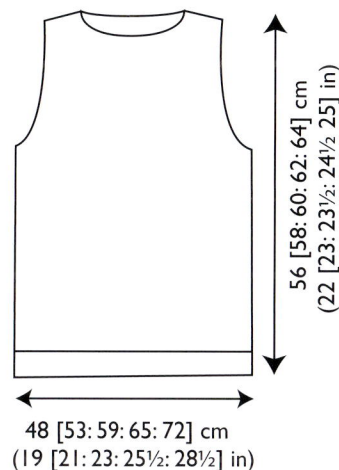

ERISKAY

● ● ●

	S	M	L	XL	XXL	
To fit bust	81-86	91-97	102-107	112-117	122-127	cm
	32-34	36-38	40-42	44-46	48-50	in

Rowan Valley Tweed

		8	8	9	10	12	x 50gm

(photographed in Malham 101)

Needles

1 pair 2¼mm (no 13) (US 1) needles
1 pair 3mm (no 11) (US 2/3) needles
Cable needle

Tension

37 sts and 39 rows to 10 cm measured over patt using 3mm (US 2/3) needles.

SPECIAL ABBREVIATIONS

C4B = slip next 2 sts onto cable needle and leave at back of work, K2, then K2 from cable needle; **C4F** = slip next 2 sts onto cable needle and leave at front of work, K2, then K2 from cable needle; **Cr4L** = slip next st onto cable needle and leave at front of work, K1, P2, then K1 from cable needle; **Cr4R** = slip next 3 sts onto cable needle and leave at back of work, K1, then P2, K1 across 3 sts on cable needle; **Tw2L** = K into back of second st on left needle, K tog tbl first 2 sts on left needle and slip both

44 [45: 46: 46: 46] cm
(17½ [17½: 18: 18: 18] in)

56 [58: 60: 62: 64] cm
(22 [23: 23½: 24½: 25] in)

48 [53: 59: 65: 72] cm
(19 [21: 23: 25½: 28½] in)

SLEEVE CHART

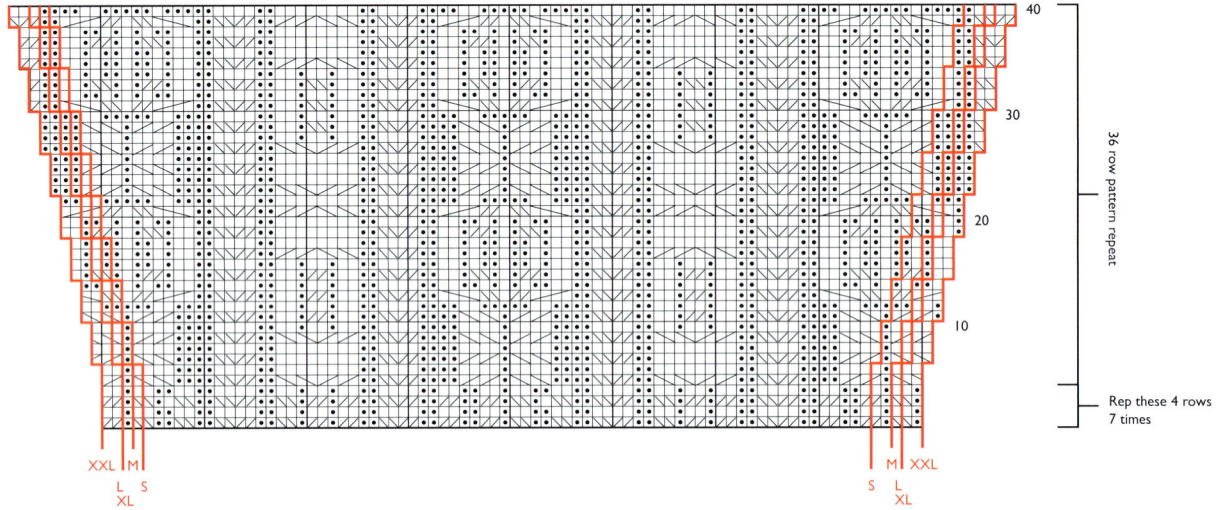

40

30

20

10

36 row pattern repeat

Rep these 4 rows
7 times

XXL M
L S
XL

S M XXL
L
XL

BODY CHART

KEY

☐ K on RS, P on WS   • P on RS, K on WS   ◤◥ Tw2L   ◤◥ Tw2R   ◢◣ C4F   ◢◣ C4B   ◢◣ Cr4R   ◢◣ Cr4L

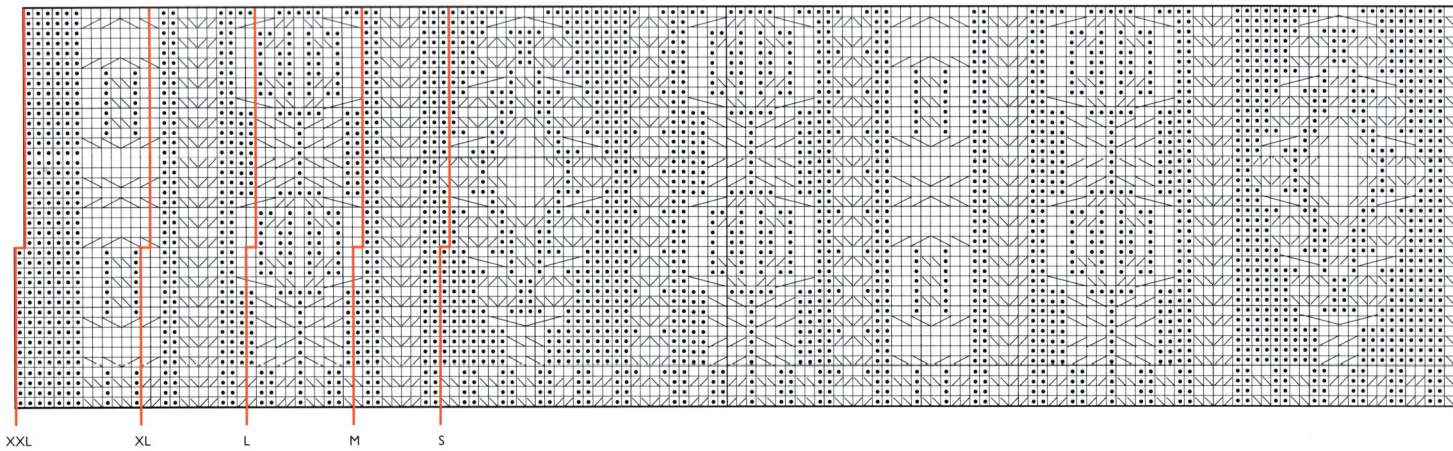

XXL   XL   L   M   S

Shape shoulders and back neck

Keeping patt correct, cast off 4 [4: 5: 6: 6] sts at beg of next 2 rows, then 4 [5: 5: 6: 6] sts at beg of foll 2 rows. 110 [116: 124: 132: 144] sts.

Next row (RS): Cast off 4 [5: 5: 6: 7] sts, patt until there are 24 [26: 28: 31: 34] sts on right needle and turn, leaving rem sts on a holder.

Work each side of neck separately.

Dec 1 st at neck edge of next 6 rows **and at same time** cast off 4 [5: 5: 6: 7] sts at beg of 2nd and foll 1 [2: 1: 2: 2] alt rows, then 5 [-: 6: -: -] sts at beg of foll 1 [-: 1: -: -] alt row.

Work 1 row.

Cast off rem 5 [5: 6: 7: 7] sts.

With RS facing, slip centre 54 [54: 58: 58: 62] sts onto a holder (for neckband), rejoin yarn and patt to end.

Complete to match first side, reversing shapings.

FRONT

Work as given for back until 16 [16: 20: 20: 24] rows less have been worked than on back to beg of shoulder shaping, ending with RS facing for next row.

Shape front neck

Next row (RS): Patt 42 [46: 51: 57: 63] sts and turn, leaving rem sts on a holder.

Work each side of neck separately.

Keeping patt correct, dec 1 st at neck edge of next 6 rows, then on foll 4 [4: 6: 6: 8] alt rows. 32 [36: 39: 45: 49] sts.

Work 1 row, ending with RS facing for next row.

Shape shoulder

Cast off 4 [4: 5: 6: 6] sts at beg of next and foll 4 [0: 4: 5: 1] alt rows, then 5 [5: 6: -: 7] sts at beg of foll 1 [5: 1: -: 4] alt rows **and at same time** dec 1 st at neck edge of next and foll 4th row.

Work 1 row.

Cast off rem 5 [5: 6: 7: 7] sts.

With RS facing, slip centre 42 sts onto a holder (for neckband), rejoin yarn and patt to end.

Complete to match first side, reversing shapings.

SLEEVES

Using 2¼mm (US 1) needles cast on 71 [75: 77: 77: 81] sts.

Beg and ending rows as indicated, cont in patt from chart for sleeve as folls:

Work chart rows 1 to 4, 7 times, ending with RS facing for next row.

Change to 3mm (US 2/3) needles.

Now repeating chart rows 5 to 40 **throughout**, cont as folls:

Inc 1 st at each end of 3rd and every foll 4th row to

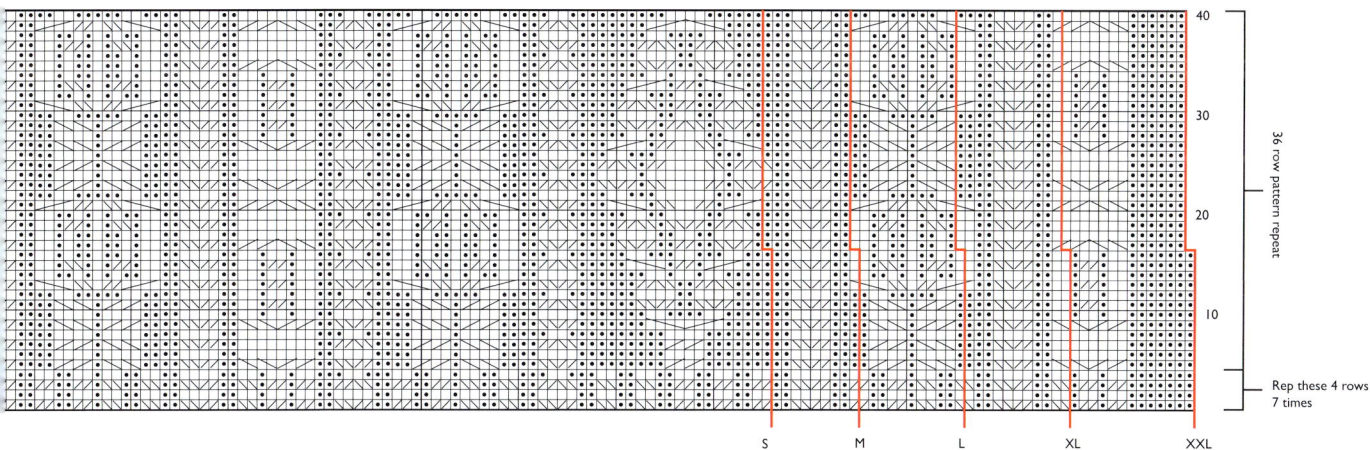

36 row pattern repeat

Rep these 4 rows 7 times

S   M   L   XL   XXL

40

30

20

10

91 [97: 107: 125: 135] sts, then on every foll 6th row until there are 119 [125: 131: 137: 143] sts, taking inc sts into patt.
Cont straight until sleeve meas 44 [45: 46: 46: 46] cm, ending with RS facing for next row.

Shape top
Keeping patt correct, cast off 9 [11: 13: 15: 17] sts at beg of next 2 rows.
101 [103: 105: 107: 109] sts.
Dec 1 st at each end of next 5 rows, then on every foll alt row until 59 sts rem, then on foll 13 rows, ending with RS facing for next row.
33 sts.
Cast off 5 sts at beg of next 2 rows.
Cast off rem 23 sts.

MAKING UP
Press as described on the information page.
Join right shoulder seam using back stitch, or mattress stitch if preferred.

Neckband
With RS facing and using 2¼mm (US 1) needles, pick up and knit 19 [19: 23: 23: 25] sts down left side of front neck, K across 42 sts on front holder as folls: K2, (K2tog, K2) 10 times, pick up and knit 19 [19: 22: 22: 25] sts up right side of front neck, and 7 sts down right side of back neck, K across 54 [54: 58: 58: 62] sts on back holder as folls: K2, (K2tog, K2) 13 [13: 14: 14: 15] times, then pick up and knit 7 sts up left side of back neck.
125 [125: 135: 135: 143] sts.
Row 1 (WS): K1, *P1, K1, rep from * to end.
Row 2: P1, *K1, P1, rep from * to end.
These 2 rows form rib.
Cont in rib for a further 3 rows, ending with RS facing for next row.
Cast off in rib.
Join left shoulder and neckband seam. Join side seams. Join sleeve seams. Insert sleeves into armholes.

S O A Y

● ● ●

To fit bust	S	M	L	XL	XXL	
	81-86	91-97	102-107	112-117	122-127	cm
	32-34	36-38	40-42	44-46	48-50	in

Rowan Felted Tweed

	7	8	9	10	11	× 50g

(photographed in Scree 165)

Needles
1 pair 2¾mm (no 12) (US 2) needles
1 pair 3¼mm (no 10) (US 3) needles
Cable needle

Tension
29 sts and 37 rows to 10 cm measured over patt using 3¼mm (US 3) needles.

SPECIAL ABBREVIATIONS
C4B = slip next 2 sts onto cable needle and leave at back of work, K2, then K2 from cable needle; **C4F** = slip next 2 sts onto cable needle and leave at front of work, K2, then K2 from cable needle; **Tw2L** = K into back of second st on left needle, K tog tbl first 2 sts on left needle and slip

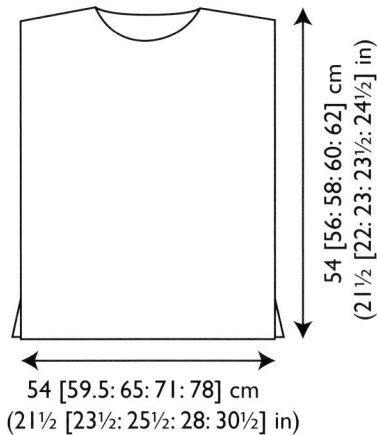

54 [56: 58: 60: 62] cm
(21½ [22: 23: 23½: 24½] in)

54 [59.5: 65: 71: 78] cm
(21½ [23½: 25½: 28: 30½] in)

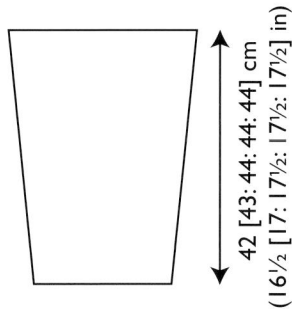

42 [43: 44: 44: 44] cm
(16½ [17: 17½: 17½: 17½] in)

both sts off left needle together; **Tw2R** = K2tog leaving sts on left needle, K first st again and slip both sts off left needle together.

BACK
Using 2¾mm (US 2) needles cast on 138 [154: 170: 188: 208] sts.
Beg and ending rows as indicated and noting that chart row 1 is a **WS** row, cont in patt from chart for body as folls:
Row 1 (WS): (K1, P1) twice, K1, work next 128 [144: 160: 178: 198] sts as row 1 of chart, K1, (P1, K1) twice.
Row 2: K2, P1, K1, P1, work next 128 [144: 160: 178: 198] sts as row 2 of chart, P1, K1, P1, K2.
Rep last 2 rows 10 times more, ending with **WS** facing for next row.
Place markers at both ends of last row (to denote top of side seam openings).
Change to 3¼mm (US 3) needles.
Now working all sts in patt from chart and repeating chart rows 3 to 34 **throughout**, cont as folls:
Inc 1 st at each end of 10th and 8 foll 10th rows, taking inc sts into patt. 156 [172: 188: 206: 226] sts.
Cont straight until back meas 51 [53: 55: 57: 59] cm, ending with RS facing

for next row.
Shape shoulders and back neck
Keeping patt correct, cast off 7 [8: 9: 10: 12] sts at beg of next 2 rows, then 7 [8: 9: 11: 12] sts at beg of foll 2 rows. 128 [140: 152: 164: 178] sts.
Next row (RS): Cast off 7 [8: 9: 11: 12] sts, patt until there are 37 [42: 46: 50: 55] sts on right needle and turn, leaving rem sts on a holder.
Work each side of neck separately.
Dec 1 st at neck edge of next 6 rows **and at same time** cast off 7 [9: 10: 11: 12] sts at beg of 2nd and foll 0 [2: 2: 2: 2] alt rows, then 8 [-: -: -: -] sts at beg of foll 2 [-: -: -: -] alt rows.
Work 1 row.
Cast off rem 8 [9: 10: 11: 13] sts.
With RS facing, slip centre 40 [40: 42: 42: 44] sts onto a holder (for neckband), rejoin yarn and patt to end.
Complete to match first side, reversing shapings.

FRONT
Work as given for back until 10 [10: 14: 14: 18] rows less have been worked than on back to beg of shoulder shaping, ending with RS facing for next row.
Shape front neck
Next row (RS): Patt 63 [71: 79: 88: 98] sts and turn, leaving rem sts on a holder.
Work each side of neck separately.
Keeping patt correct, dec 1 st at neck edge of next 8 rows, then on foll 0 [0: 2: 2: 2] alt rows, then on 0 [0: 0: 0: 1] foll 4th row.
55 [63: 69: 78: 87] sts.
Work 1 row, ending with RS facing for next row.
Shape shoulder
Cast off 7 [8: 9: 10: 12] sts at beg of next and foll 3 [2: 2: 0: 5] alt rows, then 8 [9: 10: 11: -] sts at beg of foll 2 [3: 3: 5: -] alt rows **and at same time** dec 1 st at neck edge of next [next: 3rd: 3rd: 3rd] and foll 1 [1: 0: 0: 0] alt row, then on foll 4th row.
Work 1 row.
Cast off rem 8 [9: 10: 11: 13] sts.
With RS facing, slip centre 30 sts onto a holder (for neckband), rejoin yarn and patt to end.
Complete to match first side, reversing shapings.

SLEEVES
Using 2¾mm (US 2) needles cast on 56 [58: 60: 60: 64] sts.
Beg and ending rows as indicated and noting that chart row 1 is a **WS** row, cont in patt from chart for sleeve as folls:
Work chart rows 1 and 2, 11 times, ending with **WS** facing for next row.
Change to 3¼mm (US 3) needles.
Now repeating chart rows 3 to 34 **throughout**, cont as folls:
Inc 1 st at each end of 6th [4th: 4th: 4th: 4th] and 0 [0: 4: 13: 16] foll 4th rows, then on 13 [13: 11: 5: 3] foll 6th rows, taking inc sts into cable panel and then into rev st st. 84 [86: 92: 98: 104] sts.
Work 3 [5: 1: 1: 1] rows, ending after chart row 25 and with RS facing for next row.

47

BODY CHART

KEY

☐ K on RS, P on WS   • P on RS, K on WS   ◫ Tw2R   ◫ Tw2L   ◫ C4B   ◫ C4F

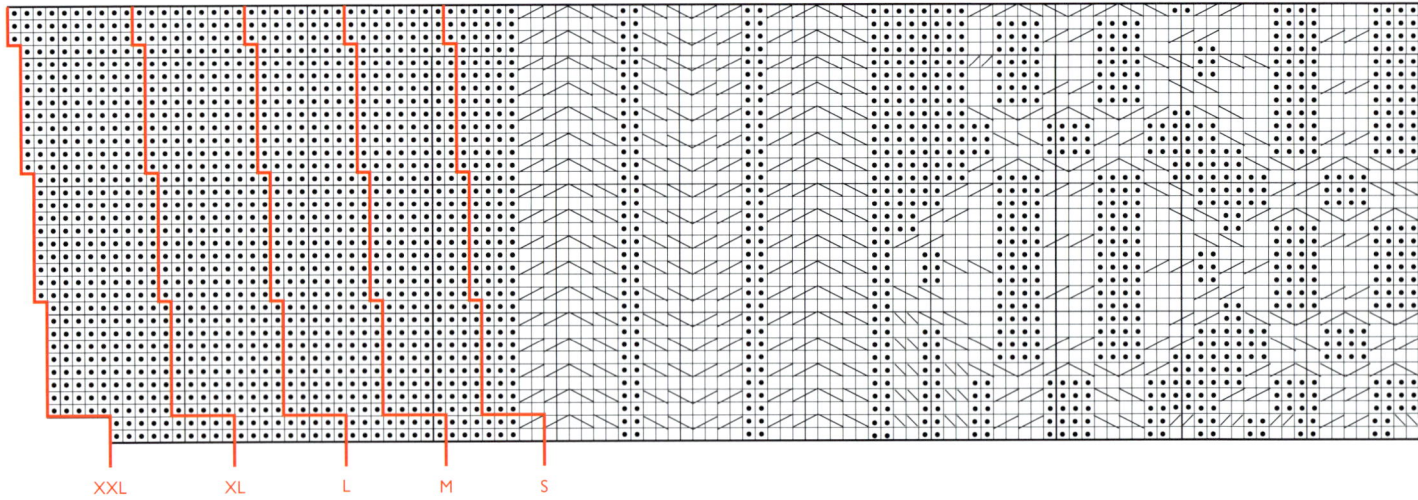

XXL   XL   L   M   S

SLEEVE CHART

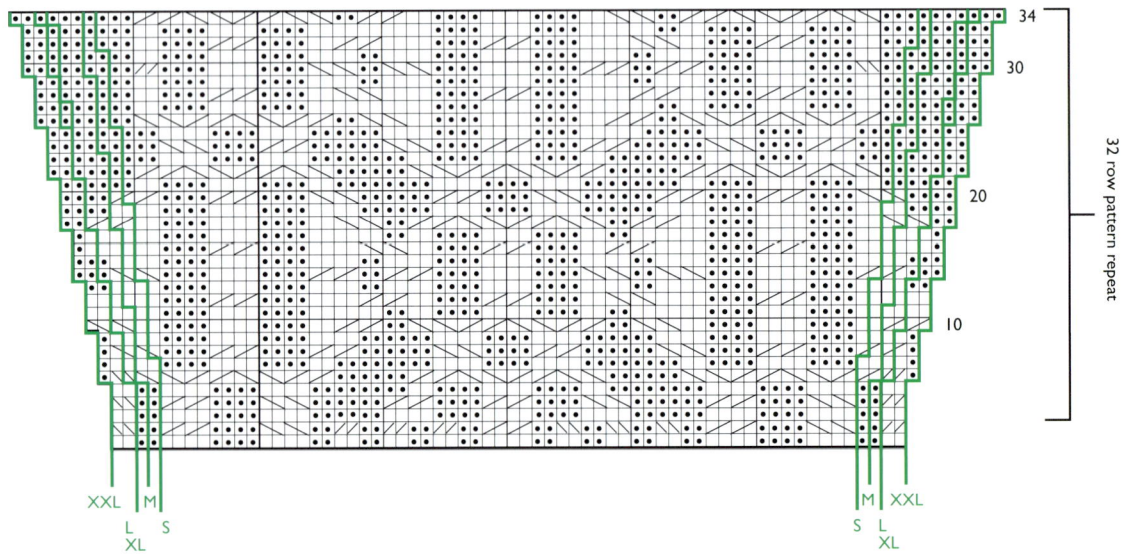

34
30
20
10

32 row pattern repeat

XXL M
L S
XL

S M XXL
L
XL

Chart labels: 34, 30, 20, 10

32 row pattern repeat

S M L XL XXL

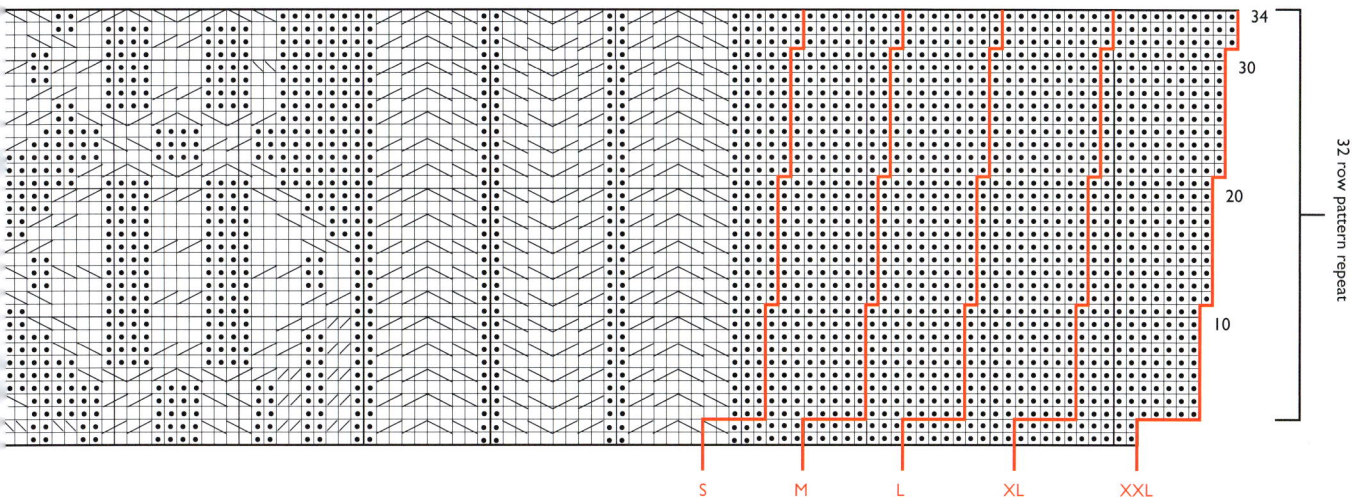

Next row (RS): (Inc in first st) 0 [1: 0: 0: 0] times, K to last 0 [1: 0: 0: 0] st, (inc in last st) 0 [1: 0: 0: 0] times. 84 [88: 92: 98: 104] sts.

Next row: Purl.

Now work in patt for top of sleeve as folls:

Row 1 (RS): (Inc in first st) 1 [0: 0: 0: 0] times, K1 [4: 0: 3: 2], (C4F) 0 [0: 0: 0: 1] times, (P2, C4F) 0 [0: 1: 1: 1] times, C4B, *P2, C4B, C4F, P2, C4F, C4B, rep from * to last 18 [20: 2: 5: 8] sts, P2, (C4B) 1 [1: 0: 0: 1] times, (C4F, P2, C4F) 1 [1: 0: 0: 0] times, K1 [4: 0: 3: 2], (inc in last st) 1 [0: 0: 0: 0] times.
86 [88: 92: 98: 104] sts.

Row 2: P7 [8: 0: 3: 6], *K2, P8, rep from * to last 9 [0: 2: 5: 8] sts, K2 [0: 2: 2: 2], P7 [0: 0: 3: 6].

These 2 rows form patt for rest of sleeve (and, for size S, cont sleeve shaping).

Cont in patt as now set, inc 1 st at each end of 7th [3rd: next: next: next] and 2 [4: 5: 5: 5] foll 8th [6th: 6th: 6th: 6th] rows, taking inc sts into patt. 92 [98: 104: 110: 116] sts.

Cont straight until sleeve meas 42 [43: 44: 44: 44] cm, ending with RS facing for next row.
Cast off.

MAKING UP
Press as described on the information page.
Join right shoulder seam using back stitch, or mattress stitch if preferred.

Neckband
With RS facing and using 2¾mm (US 2) needles, pick up and knit 19 [19: 21: 21: 23] sts down left side of front neck, K across 30 sts on front holder dec 1 st at centre, pick up and knit 19 [19: 21: 21: 23] sts up right side of front neck, and 7 sts down right side of back neck. K across 40 [40: 42: 42: 44] sts on back holder dec 2 sts evenly, then pick up and knit 7 sts up left side of back neck. 119 [119: 125: 125: 131] sts.

Row 1 (WS): K1, *P1, K1, rep from * to end.
Row 2: P1, *K1, P1, rep from * to end.
These 2 rows form rib.
Cont in rib for a further 3 rows, ending with RS facing for next row.
Cast off in rib.

Join left shoulder and neckband seam. Mark points along side seam edges 17 [18: 19: 20: 21] cm either side of shoulder seams and sew sleeves to back and front between these points. Join side and sleeve seams, leaving side seams open below markers (for side seam openings).

BUTE

● ● ●

	S	M	L	XL	XXL	
To fit bust	81-86	91-97	102-107	112-117	122-127	cm
	32-34	36-38	40-42	44-46	48-50	in

Rowan Felted Tweed

	8	9	10	11	13	× 50gm

(photographed in Scree 165)

Needles
1 pair 2¾mm (no 12) (US 2) needles
1 pair 3¼mm (no 10) (US 3) needles
Cable needle

Pattern note
The body chart is split into 4 sections, the first half on pages 54 & 55, with the top sections being on pages 52 & 53. If you wish to have a pdf of this chart then please email info@mariewallin.com

Buttons - 6 × TGB119 from Textile Garden – www.textilegarden.com

Tension
31 sts and 34½ rows to 10 cm measured over patt using 3¼mm (US 3) needles.

SPECIAL ABBREVIATIONS
Tw2L = K into back of second st on left needle, K tog tbl first 2 sts on left needle and slip both sts off left needle together; **Tw2R** = K2tog leaving sts on left needle, K first st again and slip both sts off left needle together; **Cr2L** = sl 2 sts onto cable needle and leave at front of work, P next st, K2 from cable needle; **Cr2R** = sl 1 st onto cable needle and leave at back of work, K2 then P1 from cable needle; **C4B** = sl 2 sts onto cable needle and hold at back of work, K2, then K2 from cable needle; **C4F** = sl 2 sts onto cable needle and hold at front of work, K2, then K2 from cable needle.

BACK
Using 2¾mm (US 2) needles cast on 182 [198: 216: 236: 258] sts.
Work in g st for 5 rows, ending with **WS** facing for next row.
Change to 3¼mm (US 3) needles.
Noting that row 1 of chart is a **WS** row and beg and ending rows as indicated, now work in patt from chart for body as folls:
Work chart rows 1 to 61, thus ending with RS facing for next row.
142 [158: 176: 196: 218] sts.
Cont straight until back meas 40 [41: 42: 43: 44] cm, ending with RS facing

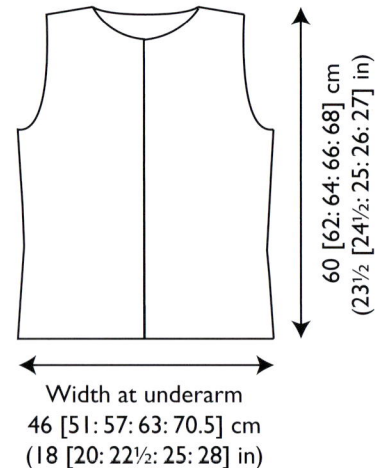

60 [62: 64: 66: 68] cm
(23½ [24½: 25: 26: 27] in)

Width at underarm
46 [51: 57: 63: 70.5] cm
(18 [20: 22½: 25: 28] in)

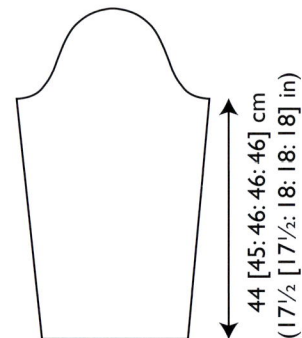

44 [45: 46: 46: 46] cm
(17½ [17½: 18: 18: 18] in)

for next row.

Shape armholes

Note: Armhole shaping is NOT shown on chart.
Keeping patt correct, cast off 4 [6: 8: 10: 12] sts at beg of next 2 rows.
134 [146: 160: 176: 194] sts.
Dec 1 st at each end of next 5 [7: 7: 9: 11] rows, then on foll
6 [7: 9: 11: 12] alt rows. 112 [118: 128: 136: 148] sts.
Cont straight until armhole meas 17 [18: 19: 20: 21] cm, ending with RS
facing for next row. (**Note**: Once chart row 177 has been completed, rep
chart rows 178 and 179 as required.)

Shape shoulders and back neck

Keeping patt correct, cast off 4 [5: 5: 6: 7] sts at beg of next 2 rows, then
5 [5: 6: 6: 7] sts at beg of foll 2 rows. 94 [98: 104: 112: 120] sts.
Next row (RS): Cast off 5 [5: 6: 7: 7] sts, patt until there are
19 [21: 22: 25: 28] sts on right needle and turn, leaving rem sts on a
holder.
Work each side of neck separately.
Dec 1 st at neck edge of next 4 rows **and at same time** cast off
5 [5: 6: 7: 8] sts at beg of 2nd row, then 5 [6: 6: 7: 8] sts at beg of foll alt row.
Work 1 row.
Cast off rem 5 [6: 6: 7: 8] sts.
With RS facing, slip centre 46 [46: 48: 48: 50] sts onto a holder, rejoin yarn
and patt to end.
Complete to match first side, reversing shapings.

LEFT FRONT

Using 2¾mm (US 2) needles cast on 92 [100: 109: 119: 130] sts.
Work in g st for 5 rows, ending with **WS** facing for next row.
Change to 3¼mm (US 3) needles.
Noting that row 1 of chart is a WS row and beg and ending rows as
indicated, now work in patt from chart for body as folls:
Row 1 (WS): K1, work 91 [99: 108: 118: 129] sts as row 1 of chart.
Row 2: Work 91 [99: 108: 118: 129] sts as row 2 of chart, K1.
These 2 rows set sts from chart, with 1 st in g st at left front opening
edge.
Cont as set until chart row 61 has been worked, ending with RS facing
for next row. 72 [80: 89: 99: 110] sts.
Cont straight until left front matches back to beg of armhole shaping,
ending with RS facing for next row.

Shape armhole

Keeping patt correct, cast off 4 [6: 8: 10: 12] sts at beg of next row.
68 [74: 81: 89: 98] sts.
Work 1 row.
Dec 1 st at armhole edge of next 5 [7: 7: 9: 11] rows, then on foll
6 [7: 9: 11: 12] alt rows. 57 [60: 65: 69: 75] sts.
Cont straight until 10 [10: 14: 14: 18] rows less have been worked than
on back to beg of shoulder shaping, ending with RS facing for next row.

Shape front neck

Next row (RS): Patt 40 [43: 48: 52: 58] sts and turn, leaving rem 17 sts on

SLEEVE CHART

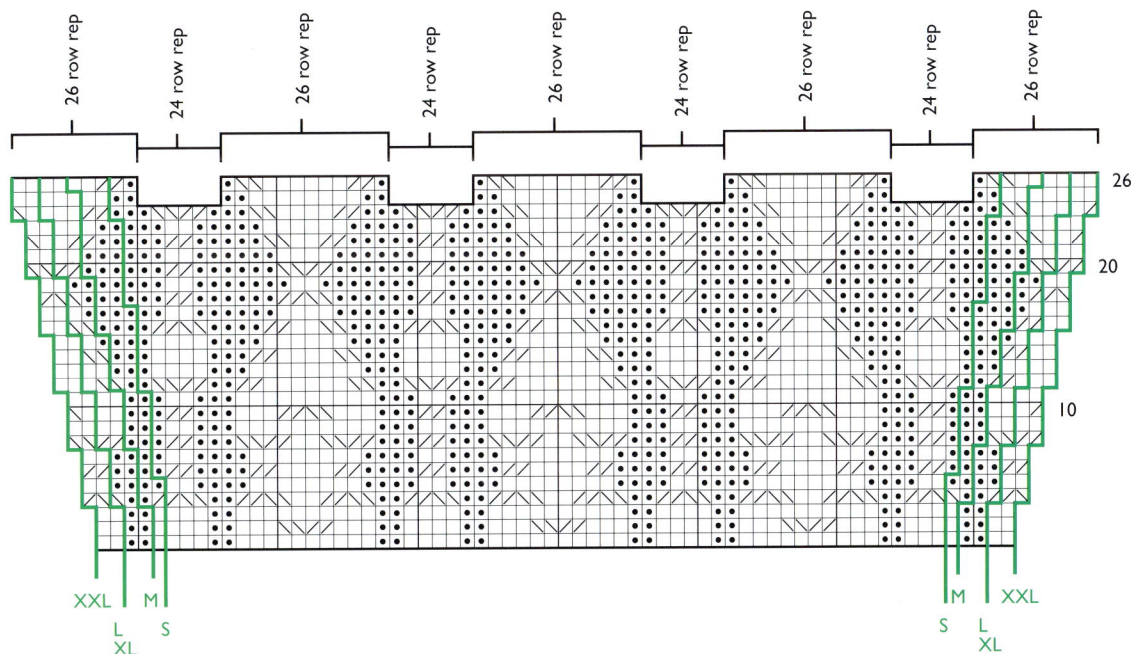

a holder (for neckband).

Keeping patt correct, dec 1 st at neck edge of next 8 rows, then on foll 0 [0: 2: 2: 2] alt rows, then on 0 [0: 0: 0: 1] foll 4th row.

32 [35: 38: 42: 47] sts.

Work 1 row, ending with RS facing for next row.

Shape shoulder

Keeping patt correct, cast off 4 [5: 6: 6: 7] sts at beg of next and foll 0 [3: 4: 1: 2] alt rows, then 5 [6: -: 7: 8] sts at beg of foll 4 [1: -: 3: 2] alt rows **and at same time** dec 1 st at neck edge of next [next: 3rd: 3rd: 3rd] and foll 1 [1: 0: 0: 0] alt row, then on foll 4th row.

Work 1 row.

Cast off rem 5 [6: 6: 7: 8] sts.

RIGHT FRONT

Using 2¾mm (US 2) needles cast on 92 [100: 109: 119: 130] sts.

Work in g st for 5 rows, ending with **WS** facing for next row.

Change to 3¼mm (US 3) needles.

Noting that row 1 of chart is a **WS** row and beg and ending rows as indicated, now work in patt from chart for body as folls:

Row 1 (WS): Work 91 [99: 108: 118: 129] sts as row 1 of chart, K1.

Row 2: K1, work 91 [99: 108: 118: 129] sts as row 2 of chart.

These 2 rows set sts from chart, with 1 st in g st at right front opening edge.

Cont as set until chart row 61 has been worked, ending with RS facing for next row. 72 [80: 89: 99: 110] sts.

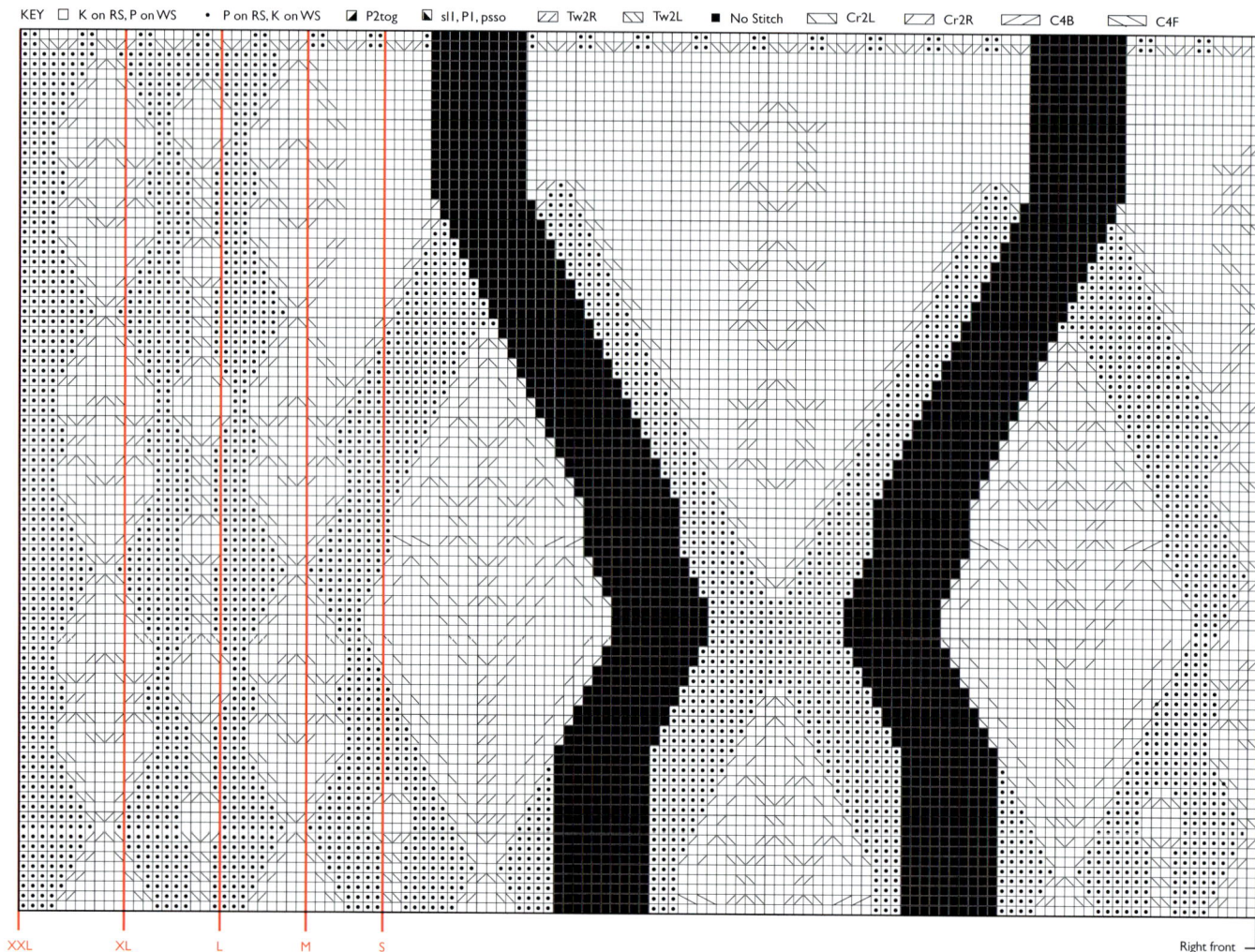

KEY ☐ K on RS, P on WS   • P on RS, K on WS   P2tog   sl1, P1, psso   Tw2R   Tw2L   ■ No Stitch   Cr2L   Cr2R   C4B   C4F

XXL   XL   L   M   S

Right front →

Complete to match left front, reversing shapings and working first row of neck shaping as folls:

Shape front neck

Next row (RS): K4, K2tog, K5, K2tog, K4 and slip these 15 sts onto a holder (for neckband), patt to end. 40 [43: 48: 52: 58] sts.

SLEEVES

Using 2¾mm (US 2) needles cast on 56 [58: 62: 62: 66] sts.

Work in g st for 5 rows, ending with **WS** facing for next row.

Change to 3¼mm (US 3) needles.

Noting that row 1 of chart is a **WS** row and beg and ending rows as indicated and repeating the 24 and the 26 row patt repeats throughout,

cont in patt from chart for sleeve as folls:

Inc 1 st at each end of 6th [4th: 4th: 4th: 4th] and 0 [4: 5: 14: 17] foll 4th rows, then on every foll 6th row until there are 100 [106: 112: 118: 124] sts, taking inc sts into patt.

Cont straight until sleeve meas 44 [45: 46: 46: 46] cm, ending with RS facing for next row.

Shape top

Keeping patt correct, cast off 4 [6: 8: 10: 12] sts at beg of next 2 rows. 92 [94: 96: 98: 100] sts.

Dec 1 st at each end of next 5 rows, then on every foll alt row until 56 sts rem, then on foll 11 rows, ending with RS facing for next row. 34 sts.

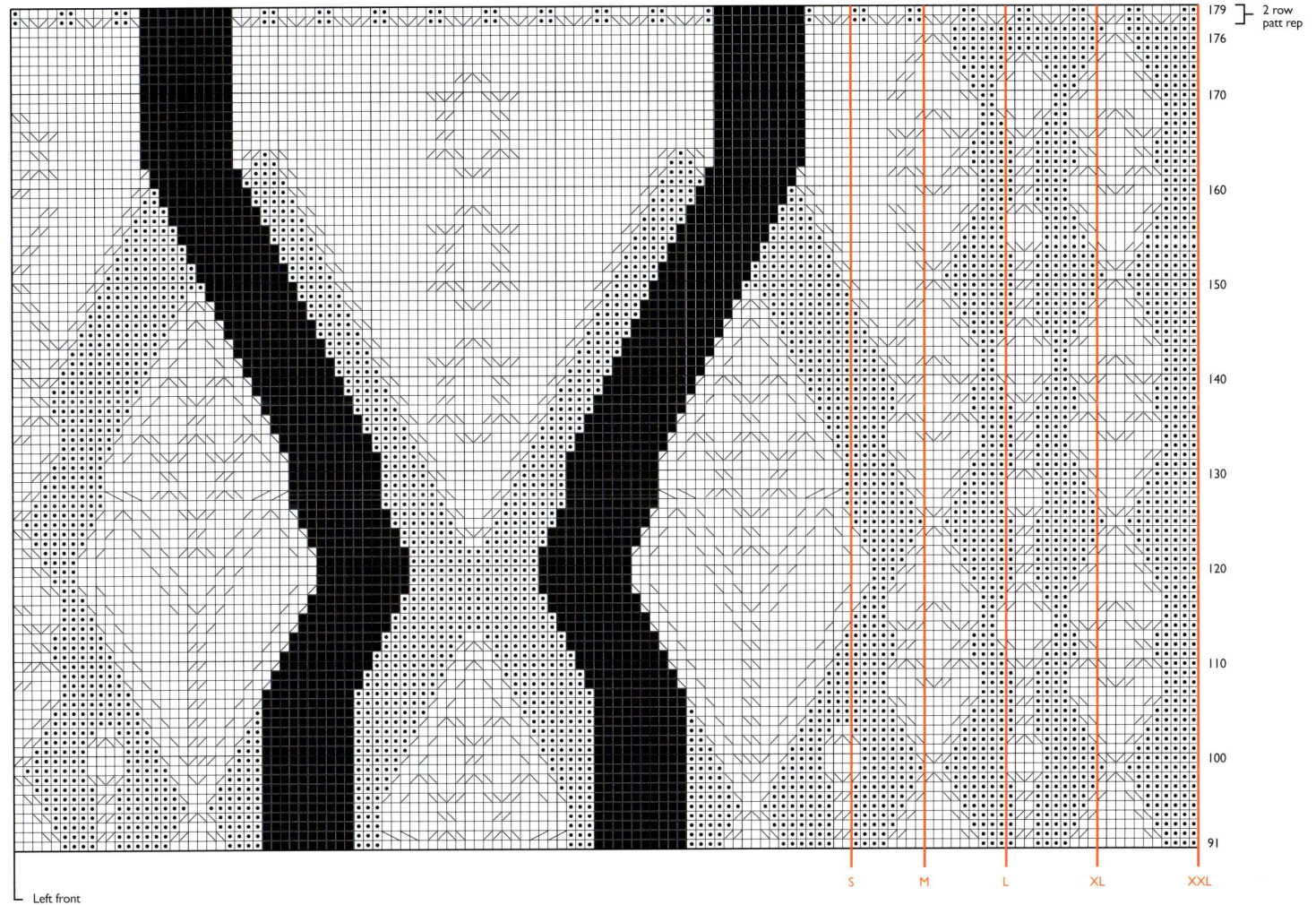

Left front

179 ⎱ 2 row patt rep
176
170
160
150
140
130
120
110
100
91

S   M   L   XL   XXL

XXL XL L M S

Right front

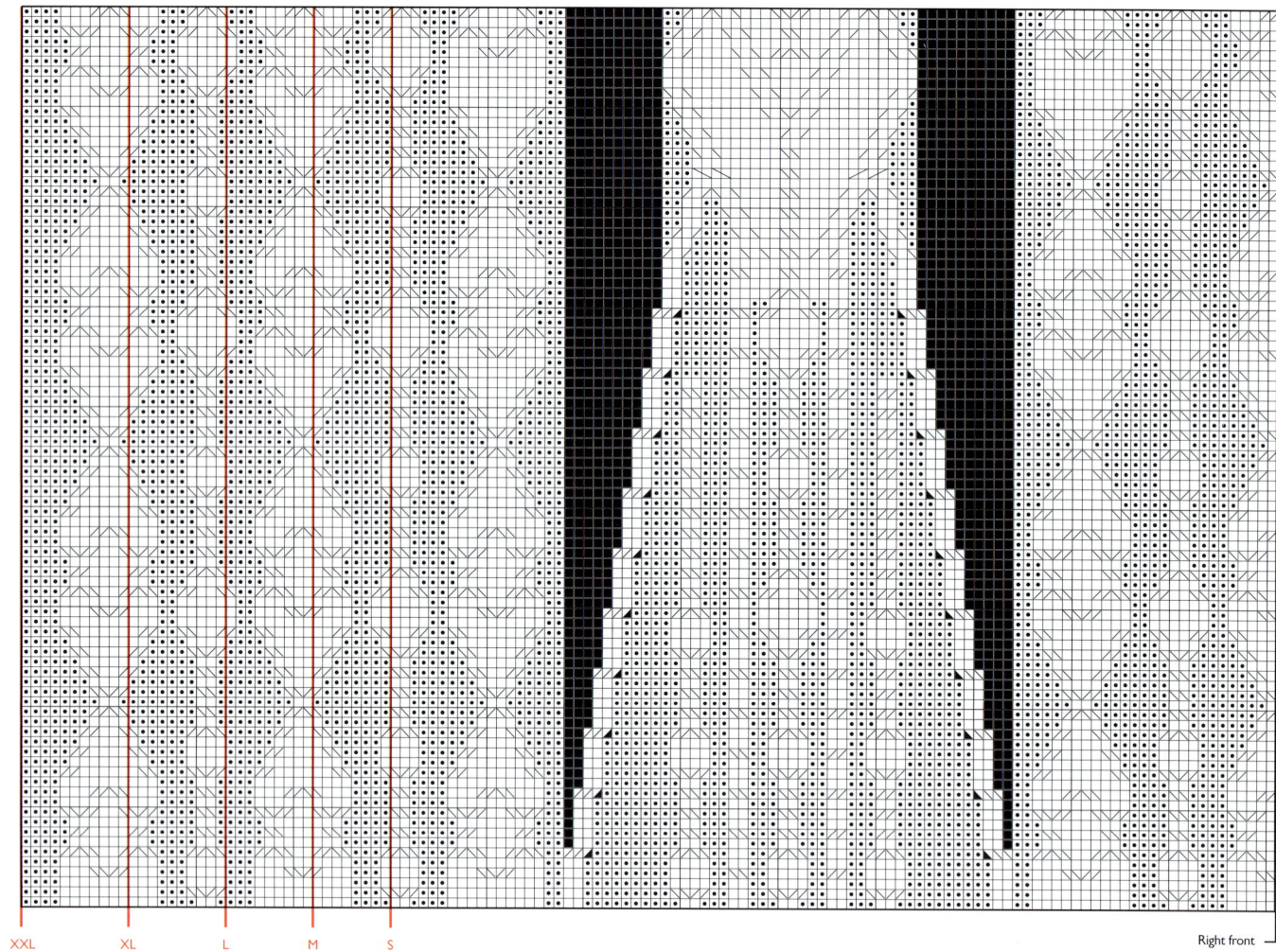

Cast off 4 sts at beg of next 4 rows.
Cast off rem 18 sts.

MAKING UP
Press as described on the information page.
Join both shoulder seams using back stitch, or mattress stitch if preferred.
Neckband
With RS facing and using 2¾mm (US 2) needles, slip 15 sts on right front holder onto right needle, rejoin yarn and pick up and knit
18 [18: 21: 21: 24] sts up right side of front neck, and 5 sts down right side

of back neck, K across 46 [46: 48: 48: 50] sts on back holder as folls:
K2 [2: 3: 3: 4], K2tog, (K8, K2tog) 4 times, K2 [2: 3: 3: 4], pick up and knit
5 sts up left side of back neck, and 18 [18: 21: 21: 24] sts down left side of front neck, then
K across 17 sts on left front holder as folls: K4, K2tog, K5, K2tog, K4.
117 [117: 125: 125: 133] sts.
Row 1 (WS): K1, *P1, K1, rep from * to end.
Row 2: K2, *P1, K1, rep from * to last st, K1.
These 2 rows form rib.
Work in rib for 2 rows more, ending with **WS** facing for next row.

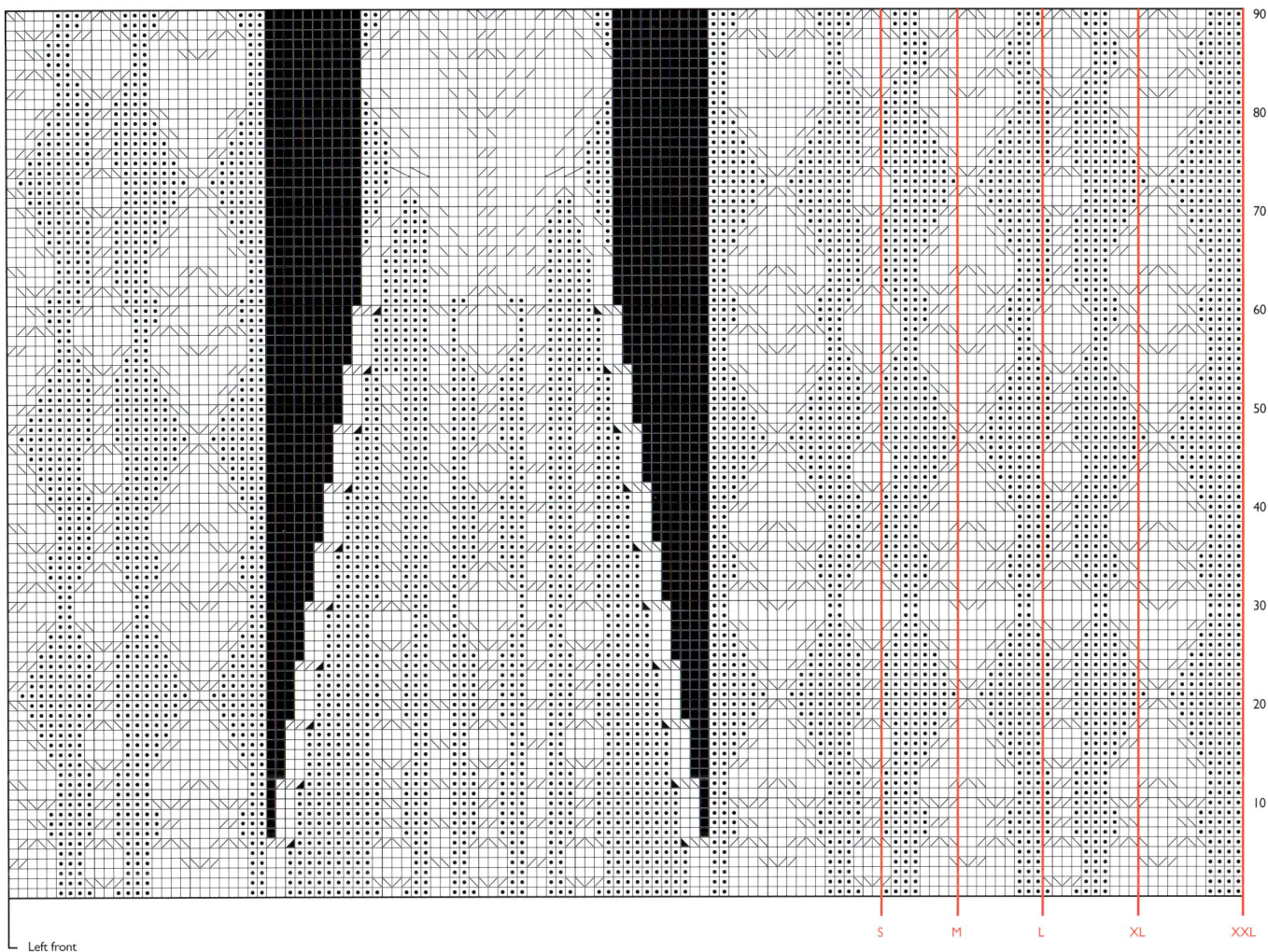

Left front

S   M   L   XL   XXL

90
80
70
60
50
40
30
20
10

Cast off in rib (on **WS**).
Button band
With RS facing and using 2¾mm (US 2) needles, pick up and knit
161 [165: 169: 175: 177] sts evenly down entire left front opening edge,
from top of neckband to cast-on edge.
Beg with row 1, work in rib as given for neckband for 4 rows, ending with
WS facing for next row.
Cast off in rib (on **WS**).

Buttonhole band
Work to match button band, picking up sts up right front opening edge
and with the addition of 6 buttonholes worked in row 2 as folls:
Row 2 (RS): Rib 56 [55: 54: 55: 57], *yrn, work 2 tog (to make a
buttonhole), rib 18 [19: 20: 21: 21], rep from * 4 times more, yrn, work
2 tog (to make 6th buttonhole), rib 3.
Join side seams. Join sleeve seams. Insert sleeves into armholes. Sew on
buttons.

BODY (knitted in one piece to armholes)
Using 2¾mm (US 2) circular needle and yarn A cast on 264 [288: 336: 360: 408] sts.
Taking care not to twist cast-on edge, work in rounds as folls:
Round 1 (RS): *K1, P1, rep from * to end.
This round forms rib.
Place marker on needle at end of last round to denote beg and end of rounds – this marker "sits" at left side seam.
Work in rib for a further 21 rounds.
Change to 3¼mm (US 3) circular needle.
Joining in and breaking off yarn B as required, using the **fairisle** technique as described on the information page and repeating the 6 st patt repeat 44 [48: 56: 60: 68] times around each round, cont in patt from chart A, which is worked entirely in st st (K every round), as folls:
Work all 22 rounds.
Break off yarn B and cont using yarn A **only**.
Next round (RS): K5 [6: 7: 7: 8], M1, (K11 [12: 14: 15: 17], M1) 23 times, K6 [6: 7: 8: 9]. 288 [312: 360: 384: 432] sts.
Repeating the 12 st patt repeat 24 [26: 30: 32: 36] times around each round and repeating the 30 round patt repeat throughout, cont in patt from chart B as folls:
Note: On chart rounds 2 and 20, there is a Tw2R at beg of the rep. End previous round (round 1 or 19) one st before end of this round so there are 2 sts to work the twist – last st of round 1 or 19, and first st of round 2 or 20.

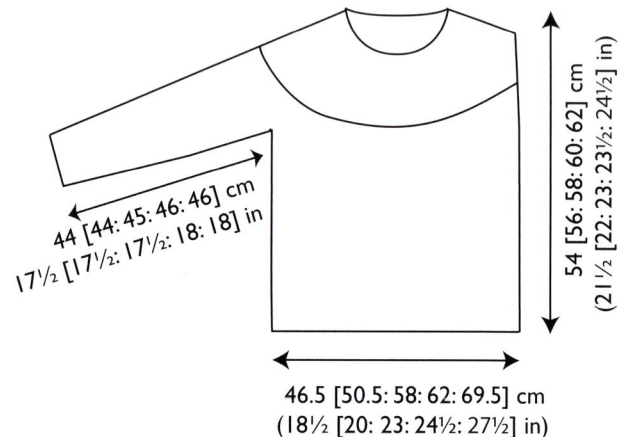

S K Y E

● ● ●

	S	M	L	XL	XXL	
To fit bust	81-86	91-97	102-107	112-117	122-127	cm
	32-34	36-38	40-42	44-46	48-50	in

Rowan Felted Tweed

A Clay 177	7	8	9	10	11	x 50gm
B Maritime 167	1	1	2	2	2	x 50gm

Needles
2¾mm (no 12) (US 2) circular needle
3¼mm (no 10) (US 3) circular needle
Set of 4 double-pointed 2¾mm (no 12) (US 2) needles
Set of 4 double-pointed 3¼mm (no 10) (US 3) needles

Tension
29 sts and 30 rows to 10 cm measured over patterned st st, 31 sts and 34½ rows to 10 cm measured over textured patt, both using 3¼mm (US 3) needles.

SPECIAL ABBREVIATIONS
Tw2L = K into back of second st on left needle, K tog tbl first 2 sts on left needle and slip both sts off left needle together; **Tw2R** = K2tog leaving sts on left needle, K first st again and slip both sts off left needle together.

44 [44: 45: 46: 46] cm
17½ [17½: 17½: 18: 18] in

54 [56: 58: 60: 62] cm
(21½ [22: 23: 23½: 24½] in)

46.5 [50.5: 58: 62: 69.5] cm
(18½ [20: 23: 24½: 27½] in)

Cont straight until body meas 26 [27: 28: 29: 30] cm.
Divide for armholes
Next round: Patt 5 sts and slip these sts onto a holder (for left underarm), patt until there are 134 [146: 170: 182: 206] sts on right needle and slip these sts onto another holder (for front), patt next 10 sts and slip these sts onto another holder (for right underarm), patt until there are 134 [146: 170: 182: 206] sts on right needle and slip these sts onto another holder (for back), patt rem 5 sts and slip these 5 sts onto same holder as first 5 sts (so there are 10 sts on left underarm holder).
Break yarn.

SLEEVES
Using set of 4 double-pointed 2¾mm (US 2) needles and yarn A cast on 52 [56: 60: 60: 62] sts.
Taking care not to twist cast-on edge, work in rounds as folls:
Work in rib as given for body for 1 round.
Place marker between first and last sts of last round to denote beg and ends of rounds – this is underarm point.
Work in rib for a further 21 rounds, inc 1 st at end of last round. 53 [57: 61: 61: 63] sts.
Change to double-pointed 3¼mm (US 3) needles.
Beg and ending rows as indicated, joining in and breaking off yarn B as required and using the **fairisle** technique as described on the information page, cont in patt from chart C, which is worked entirely in st st (K every round), as folls:
Inc 1 st at each end of 3rd and 4 [2: 0: 4: 4] foll 4th rounds, then on 0 [1: 3: 0: 0] foll 6th rounds, taking inc sts into patt. 63 [65: 69: 71: 73] sts.
Work 3 [5: 1: 3: 3] rounds, ending after chart round 22.
Break off yarn B and cont using yarn A **only**.
Next round (RS): (Inc in first st) 1 [1: 0: 1: 1] times, K4 [5: 6: 6: 5], M1, (K13 [13: 14: 14: 15], M1) 4 times, K5 [6: 7: 7: 6], (inc in last st) 1 [1: 0: 1: 1] times. 70 [72: 74: 78: 80] sts.
Beg and ending rows as indicated and repeating the 30 round patt repeat throughout, cont in patt from chart D as folls:
Inc 1 st at each end of 6th [6th: 4th: 6th: 4th] and 0 [0: 0: 0: 2] foll 4th rounds, then on every foll 6th round until there are 100 [102: 106: 110: 114] sts, taking inc sts into patt.
Cont straight until sleeve meas approx 44 [44: 45: 46: 46] cm, ending after same patt round as on body to divide for armholes row.
Next round: Patt 5 sts and slip these sts onto a holder (for underarm), patt to last 5 sts, patt rem 5 sts and slip these 5 sts onto same holder as first 5 sts (so there are 10 sts on underarm holder).
Break yarn and leave rem 90 [92: 96: 100: 104] sts on another holder.

YOKE
With RS facing and using 3¼mm (US 3) circular needle, rejoin yarn A and work across sts on left sleeve, front, right sleeve and back holders as folls:
(K1, patt to last st, K1, place marker on needle) 4 times.
448 [476: 532: 564: 620] sts. 4 markers in total – each marker is between sections from holders and these denote raglan sleeve "seams".
Keeping patt correct, cont as folls:

Next round (RS): (Sl 1, K1, psso, patt to within 2 sts of next marker, K2tog, slip marker onto right needle) 4 times.
Next round: (K1, patt to within 1 st of next marker, K1, slip marker onto right needle) 4 times.
Rep last 2 rounds 11 [12: 14: 16: 17] times more, and then first of these 2 rounds (the dec round) again. 344 [364: 404: 420: 468] sts.
Remove raglan "seam" markers and place one new marker between centre back 2 sts – this will now be new beg and end point of rounds for rest of yoke.
Break yarn.
Re-arrange sts so that rounds will now start again at centre back, rejoin yarn A with RS facing and cont as folls:
Next round (RS): K8 [5: 15: 16: 5], K2tog, (K13 [11: 10: 9: 11], K2tog 21 [27: 31: 35: 35] times, K9 [6: 15: 17: 6]. 312 [336: 372: 384: 432] sts.
Joining in and breaking off yarn B as required, using the **fairisle** technique as described on the information page and repeating the 12 st patt rep 26 [28: 31: 32: 36] times around each round, cont in patt from chart E, which is worked entirely in st st, until chart round 10 has been completed.
Chart round 11: Using yarn A, K0 [3: 6: 12: 6], (K2 [2: 1: 1: 1], K2tog, K5 [3: 3: 3: 3], sl 1, K1, psso, K2) 24 [30: 36: 36: 42] times, K0 [3: 6: 12: 6]. 264 [276: 300: 312: 348] sts.
Repeating the 12 st patt rep 22 [23: 25: 26: 29] times around each round, work chart rounds 12 to 29.
(**Note:** As number of sts decreases, change from circular needle to set of 4 double-pointed needles).
Chart round 30: Using yarn A, K0 [3: 0: 12: 12], (K2 [1: 1: 1: 1], K2tog, K3 [3: 3: 2: 3], sl 1, K1, psso, K2 [1: 2: 1: 1]) 24 [30: 30: 36: 36] times, K0 [3: 0: 12: 12]. 216 [216: 240: 240: 276] sts.
Repeating the 12 st patt rep 18 [18: 20: 20: 23] times around each round, work chart rounds 31 to 38.
Break off yarn B and cont using yarn A **only**.
Working in st st throughout (K every round), complete yoke as folls:
Work 1 round.
Next round: K0 [0: 0: 0: 12], (K1, K2tog, K3 [3: 2: 2: 1], sl 1, K1, psso, K1) 24 [24: 30: 30: 36] times, K0 [0: 0: 0: 12]. 168 [168: 180: 180: 204] sts.
Cont in st st until yoke section meas 27 [28: 29: 30: 31] cm from sts left on holders at underarms.
Next round: K7 [7: 12: 12: 12], (K1 [1: 1: 1: 0], K2tog, K1, sl 1, K1, psso, K1 [1: 0: 0: 0]) 22 [22: 26: 26: 36] times, K7 [7: 12: 12: 12]. 124 [124: 128: 128: 132] sts.
Work 2 rounds.
Work neckband
Change to 2¾mm (US 2) double-pointed needles.
Work in rib as given for body for 5 rounds.
Cast off loosely in rib.

MAKING UP
Press as described on the information page.
Join underarm seams by grafting together sets of 10 sts on underarm holders.
See information page for finishing instructions.

CHART A

6 st patt rep

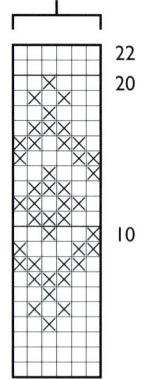

22
20

10

CHART B

12 st repeat

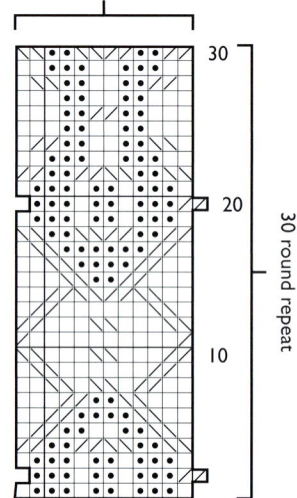

30

20

10

30 round repeat

KEY

A. ☐ Clay 177 - K on RS, P on WS
   • Clay 177 - P on RS, K on WS

B. ✕ Maritime 167

   Tw2L

   Tw2R

CHART C

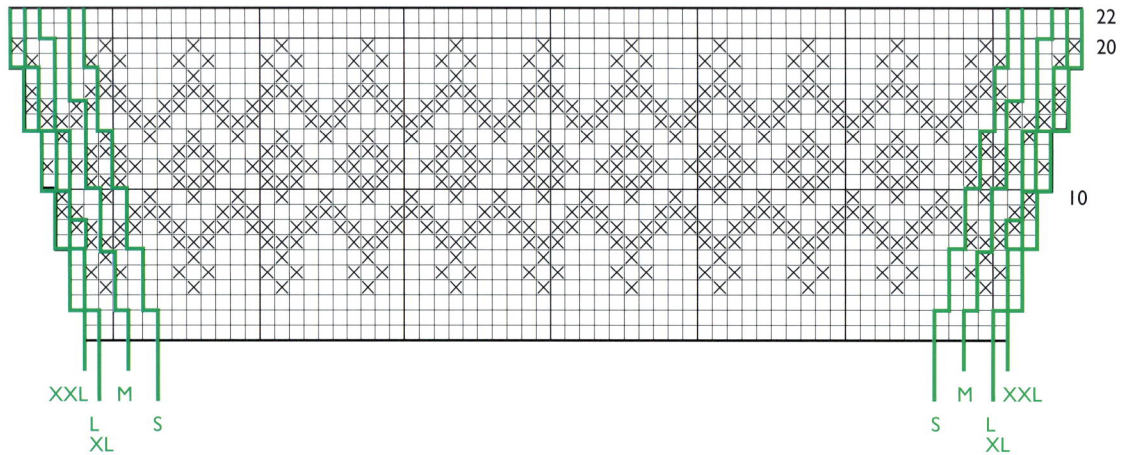

22
20

10

XXL M   S
  L
  XL

S   M XXL
      L
      XL

CHART D

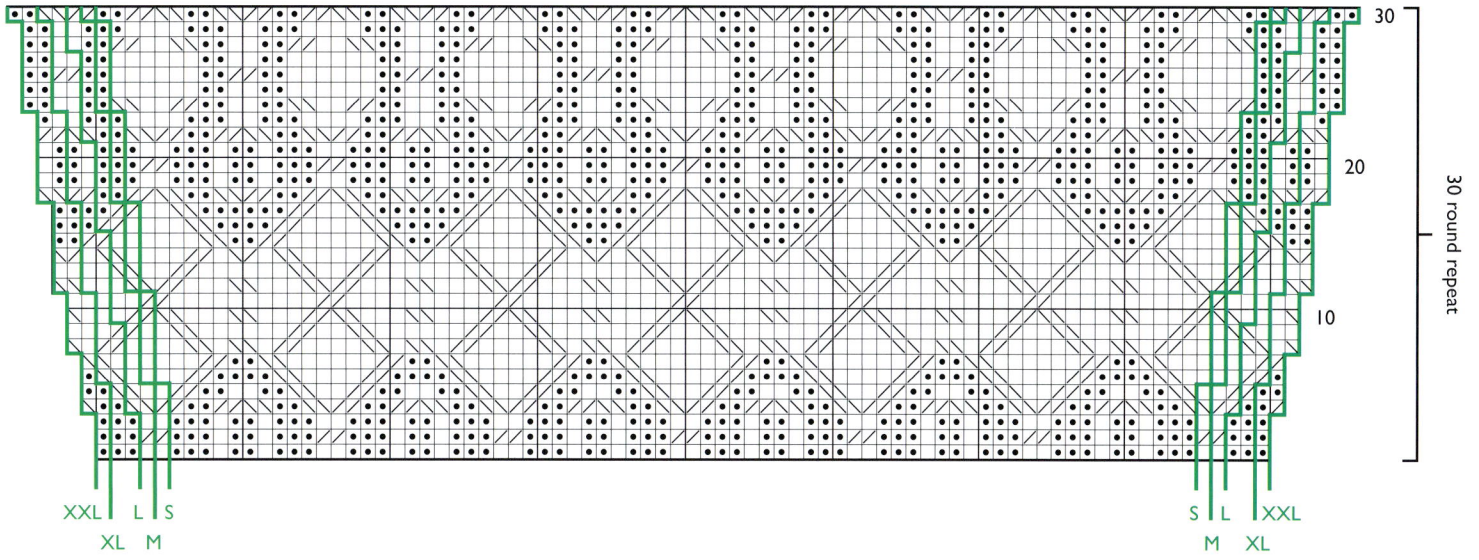

XXL   L   S
     XL M

S   L   XXL
  M   XL

30 round repeat

30

20

10

CHART E

12 st repeat

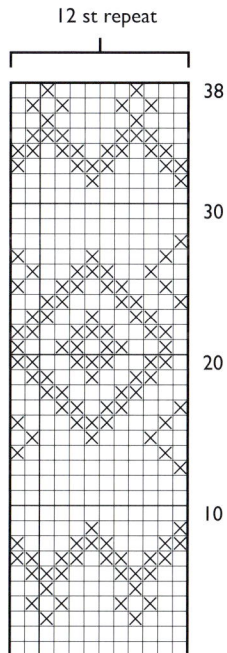

38

30

20

10

Row 20 (WS): Using yarn A, purl.

Beg and ending rows as indicated and using the **fairisle** technique as described on the information page, cont in patt from chart for body, which is worked **mainly** in st st beg with a K row, as folls:

Work chart rows 1 to 4, 7 times, then work chart rows 5 to 8 once.

Now rep chart rows 9 to 28, 5 times.

Now repeating chart rows 29 to 48 **throughout**, cont as folls:

Cont straight until back meas 59 [61: 63: 65: 67] cm, ending with RS facing for next row.

Shape shoulders and back neck

Keeping patt correct, cast off 9 [11: 12: 14: 15] sts at beg of next 2 rows, then 10 [11: 12: 14: 16] sts at beg of foll 2 rows.

135 [145: 161: 171: 187] sts.

Next row (RS): Cast off 10 [11: 13: 14: 16] sts, patt until there are 34 [38: 43: 47: 52] sts on right needle and turn, leaving rem sts on a holder. Work each side of neck separately.

Dec 1 st at neck edge of next 4 rows **and at same time** cast off 10 [11: 13: 14: 16] sts at beg of 2nd and foll alt row.

Work 1 row.

TIREE ● ●

	S	M	L	XL	XXL	
To fit bust	81-86	91-97	102-107	112-117	122-127	cm
	32-34	36-38	40-42	44-46	48-50	in

Rowan Valley Tweed

		S	M	L	XL	XXL	
A	Malham 101	5	5	6	8	9	x 50gm
B	Penyghent 104	5	6	7	8	9	x 50gm

Needles

1 pair 2¼mm (no 13) (US 1) needles
1 pair 3mm (no 11) (US 2/3) needles

Tension

32 sts and 31 rows to 10 cm measured over patterned st st using 3mm (US 2/3) needles.

BACK

Using 2¼mm (US 1) needles and yarn B cast on 173 [189: 209: 227: 249] sts.

Row 1 (RS): K1, *P1, K1, rep from * to end.
Row 2: P1, *K1, P1, rep from * to end.
These 2 rows form rib.

Work in rib for a further 17 rows, ending with **WS** facing for next row.

Change to 3mm (US 2/3) needles.

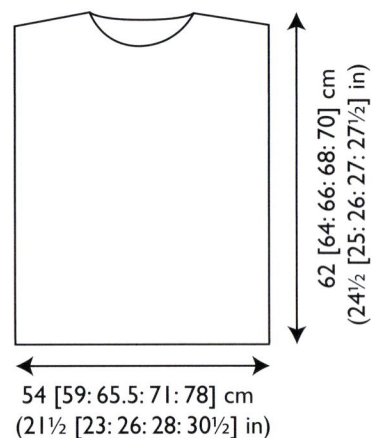

62 [64: 66: 68: 70] cm
(24½ [25: 26: 27: 27½] in)

54 [59: 65.5: 71: 78] cm
(21½ [23: 26: 28: 30½] in)

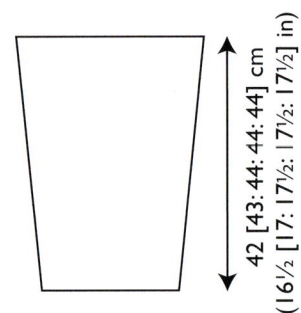

42 [43: 44: 44: 44] cm
(16½ [17: 17½: 17½: 17½] in)

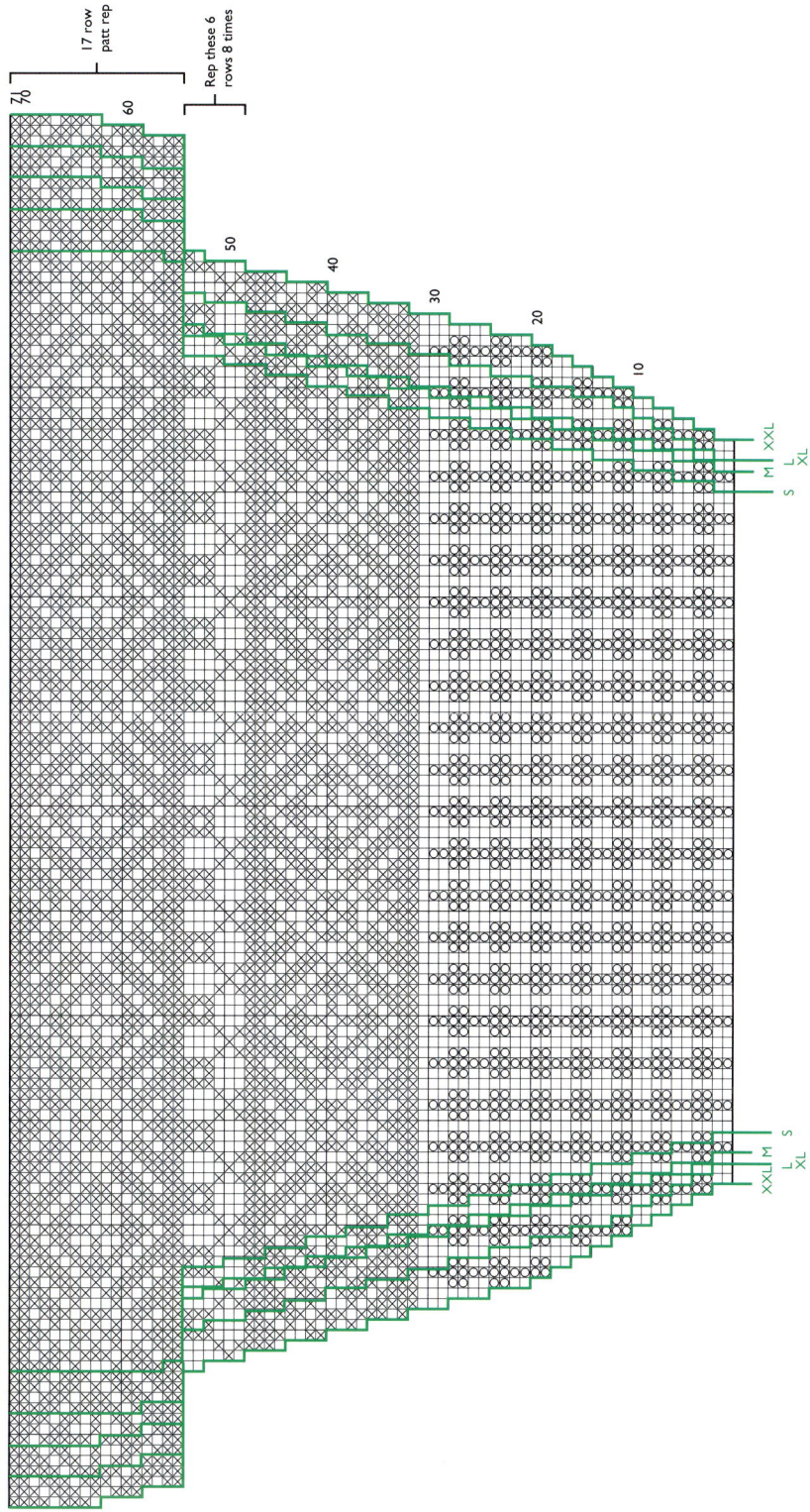

SLEEVE CHART

17 row
patt rep

Rep these 6
rows 8 times

70
60
50
40
30
20
10

S M XXL
L
XL

XXL M S
L
XL

BODY CHART

KEY

A. □ Malham 101   B. ○ Penyghent 104 - P on RS, K on WS   B. ✕ Penyghent 104

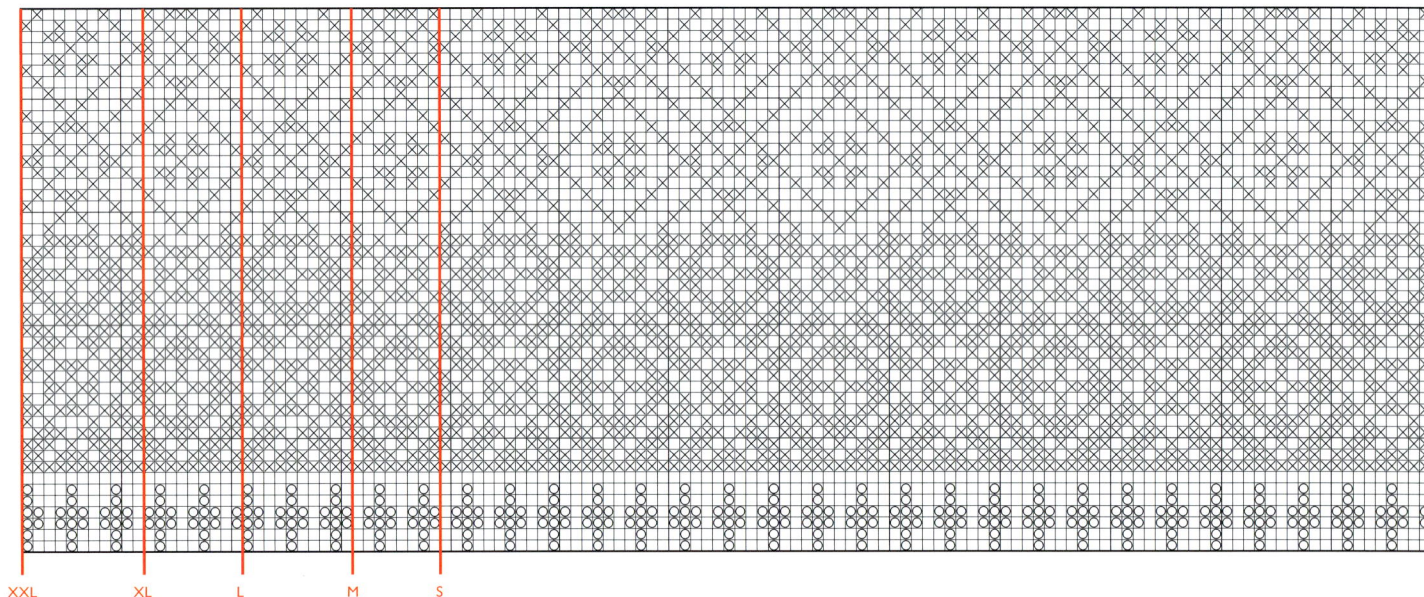

XXL   XL   L   M   S

Cast off rem 10 [12: 13: 15: 16] sts.
With RS facing, slip centre 47 [47: 49: 49: 51] sts onto a holder (for neckband), rejoin yarns and patt to end.
Complete to match first side, reversing shapings.

FRONT
Work as given for back until 8 [8: 12: 12: 16] rows less have been worked than on back to beg of shoulder shaping, ending with RS facing for next row.
Shape front neck
Next row (RS): Patt 68 [76: 86: 95: 106] sts and turn, leaving rem sts on a holder.
Work each side of neck separately.
Keeping patt correct, dec 1 st at neck edge of next 6 rows, then on foll 0 [0: 2: 2: 2] alt rows, then on 0 [0: 0: 0: 1] foll 4th row.
62 [70: 78: 87: 97] sts.
Work 1 row, ending with RS facing for next row.
Shape shoulder
Cast off 9 [11: 12: 14: 15] sts at beg of next and foll 0 [4: 1: 4: 0] alt rows,

then 10 [-: 13: -: 16] sts at beg of foll 4 [-: 3: -: 4] alt rows **and at same time** dec 1 st at neck edge of next [next: 3rd: 3rd: 3rd] and foll 1 [1: 0: 0: 0] alt row, then on foll 4th row.
Work 1 row.
Cast off rem 10 [12: 13: 15: 16] sts.
With RS facing, slip centre 37 sts onto a holder (for neckband), rejoin yarns and patt to end.
Complete to match first side, reversing shapings.

SLEEVES
Using 2¼mm (US 1) needles and yarn B cast on 61 [65: 67: 67: 71] sts.
Work in rib as given for back for 19 rows, ending with **WS** facing for next row.
Change to 3mm (US 2/3) needles.
Row 20 (WS): Using yarn A, purl.
Beg and ending rows as indicated and using the **fairisle** technique as described on the information page, cont in patt from chart for sleeve, which is worked **mainly** in st st beg with a K row, as folls:
Inc 1 st at each end of 3rd [3rd: next: next: next] and foll 0 [0: 0: 6: 10] alt

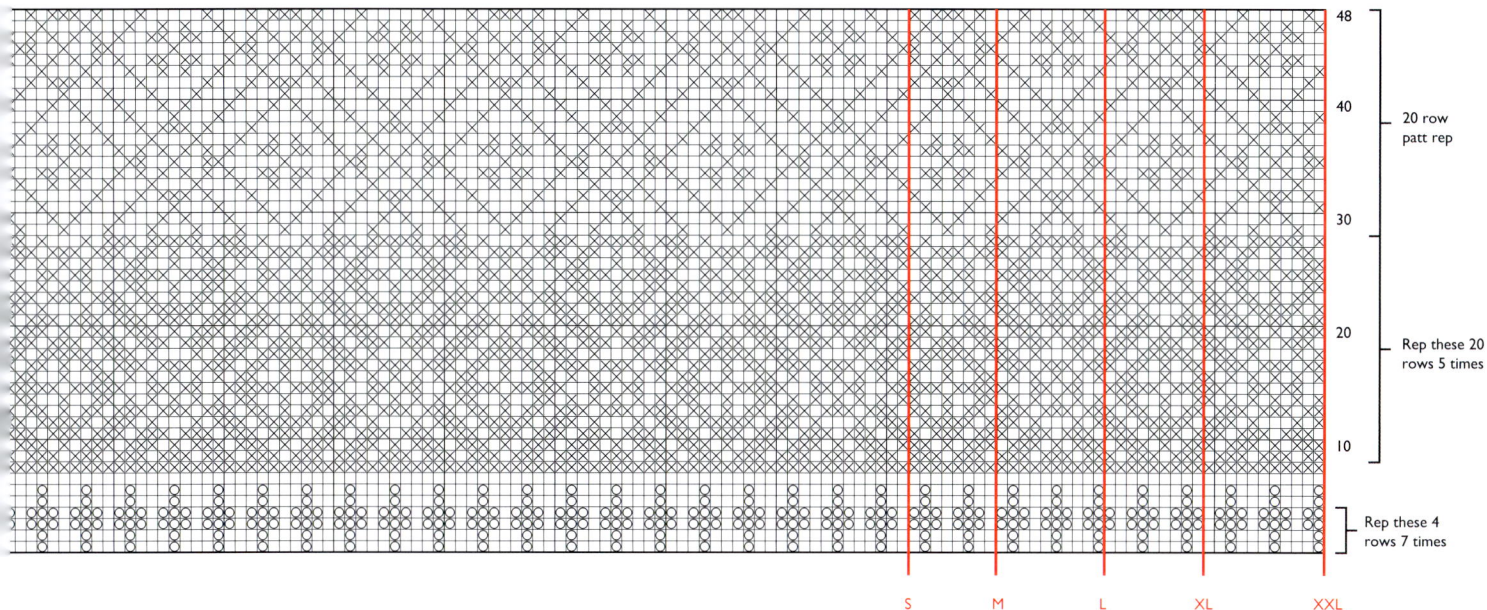

48

40

20 row
patt rep

30

20

Rep these 20
rows 5 times

10

Rep these 4
rows 7 times

S   M   L   XL   XXL

rows, then on 11 [11: 11: 8: 6] foll 4th rows, taking inc sts into patt.
85 [89: 91: 97: 105] sts.
Work 1 [1: 3: 3: 3] rows, ending after chart row 48 and with RS facing for next row.
Now repeating chart rows 49 to 54, 8 times **in total**, cont as folls:
Inc 1 st at each end of 3rd [3rd: next: next: next] and 9 [11: 11: 11: 11] foll 4th rows, then on 1 [0: 0: 0: 0] foll 6th row, taking inc sts into patt.
107 [113: 115: 121: 129] sts.
Work 3 [1: 3: 3: 3] rows, ending after 8th rep of chart row 54 and with RS facing for next row.
Now repeating chart rows 55 to 71 throughout, cont as folls:
Inc 1 st at each end of 3rd [5th: next: next: next] and 0 [0: 2: 2: 2] foll 4th rows, taking inc sts into patt. 109 [115: 121: 127: 135] sts.
Cont straight until sleeve meas 42 [43: 44: 44: 44] cm, ending with RS facing for next row.
Cast off.

MAKING UP
Press as described on the information page.

Join right shoulder seam using back stitch, or mattress stitch if preferred.
Neckband
With RS facing, using 2¼mm (US 1) needles and yarn B, pick up and knit 19 [19: 22: 22: 25] sts down left side of front neck, K across 37 sts on front holder, pick up and knit 19 [19: 22: 22: 25] sts up right side of front neck, and 5 sts down right side of back neck, K across 47 [47: 49: 49: 51] sts on back holder dec 1 st at centre, then pick up and knit 5 sts up left side of back neck. 131 [131: 139: 139: 147] sts.
Beg with row 2, work in rib as given for back for 15 rows, ending with RS facing for next row.
Cast off in rib.
Join left shoulder and neckband seam. Mark points along side seam edges 18 [18: 20: 21: 22] cm either side of shoulder seams and sew sleeves to back and front between these points. Join side and sleeve seams.

UIST

BACK

Using 2¾mm (US 2) needles and yarn A cast on
157 [171: 189: 205: 227] sts.

Row 1 (RS): K1, *P1, K1, rep from * to end.

Row 2: P1, *K1, P1, rep from * to end.

These 2 rows form rib.

Work in rib for a further 27 rows, ending with **WS** facing for next row.

Change to 3¼mm (US 3) needles.

Row 30 (WS): Using yarn A, purl.

Beg and ending rows as indicated, using the **fairisle** technique as described on the information page and repeating the 46 row patt repeat throughout, cont in patt from chart for lower section, which is worked entirely in st st beg with a K row, as folls:

Cont straight until back meas 52 [54: 56: 58: 60] cm, ending with RS facing for next row.

Next row (RS): Using yarn A K3 [5: 4: 4: 1], M1, (K15 [16: 15: 14: 16], M1) 10 [10: 12: 14: 14] times, K4 [6: 5: 5: 2]. 168 [182: 202: 220: 242] sts.

Break off yarn A and complete back using yarn B **only**.

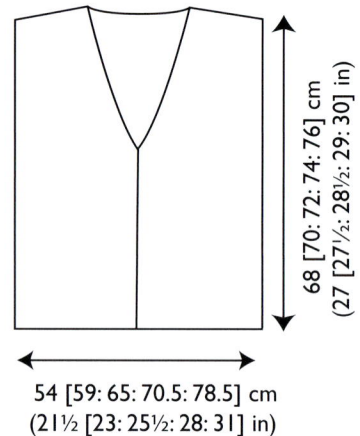

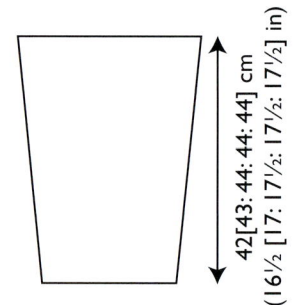

	S	M	L	XL	XXL	
To fit bust	81-86	91-97	102-107	112-117	122-127	cm
	32-34	36-38	40-42	44-46	48-50	in

Rowan Felted Tweed

A Clay 177	8	9	9	10	11	× 50gm
B Granite 191	6	6	7	7	8	× 50gm

Needles

1 pair 2¾mm (no 12) (US 2) needles
1 pair 3¼mm (no 10) (US 3) needles
2¾mm (no 12) (US 2) circular needle

Buttons – 7 × TGB 2395 from Textile Garden – www.textilegarden.com

Tension

29 sts and 30 rows to 10 cm measured over patterned st st, 31 sts and 34½ rows to 10 cm measured over yoke patt, both using 3¼mm (US 3) needles.

SPECIAL ABBREVIATIONS

Tw2L = K into back of second st on left needle, K tog tbl first 2 sts on left needle and slip both sts off left needle together; **Tw2R** = K2tog leaving sts on left needle, K first st again and slip both sts off left needle together.

54 [59: 65: 70.5: 78.5] cm
(21½ [23: 25½: 28: 31] in)

68 [70: 72: 74: 76] cm
(27 [27½: 28½: 29: 30] in)

42 [43: 44: 44: 44] cm
(16½ [17: 17½: 17½: 17½] in)

Next row (WS): Purl.

Beg and ending rows as indicated and repeating the 24 row patt repeat throughout, cont in patt from chart for yoke as folls:

Cont straight until back meas 65 [67: 69: 71: 73] cm, ending with RS facing for next row.

Shape shoulders and back neck

Keeping patt correct, cast off 9 [10: 12: 13: 15] sts at beg of next 4 rows. 132 [142: 154: 168: 182] sts.

Next row (RS): Cast off 9 [10: 12: 13: 15] sts, patt until there are 33 [37: 40: 46: 50] sts on right needle and turn, leaving rem sts on a holder. Work each side of neck separately.

Dec 1 st at neck edge of next 4 rows **and at same time** cast off 9 [11: 12: 14: 15] sts at beg of 2nd row, then 10 [11: 12: 14: 15] sts at beg of foll alt row.

Work 1 row.

Cast off rem 10 [11: 12: 14: 16] sts.

With RS facing, slip centre 48 [48: 50: 50: 52] sts onto a holder, rejoin yarn and patt to end.

Complete to match first side, reversing shapings.

POCKET LININGS (make 2)

Using 3¼mm (US 3) needles and yarn A cast on 40 [40: 42: 42: 44] sts.

Beg with a K row, work in st st for 49 rows, ending with **WS** facing for next row.

Next row (WS): P6 [6: 7: 7: 8], M1P, (P14, M1P) twice, P6 [6: 7: 7: 8]. 43 [43: 45: 45: 47] sts.

Break yarn and leave sts on a holder.

LEFT FRONT

Using 2¾mm (US 2) needles and yarn A cast on 78 [84: 94: 102: 112] sts.

Row 1 (RS): *K1, P1, rep from * to last 2 sts, K2.

Row 2: *K1, P1, rep from * to end.

These 2 rows form rib.

Work in rib for a further 27 rows, inc 0 [1: 0: 0: 1] st at beg of last row and ending with **WS** facing for next row. 78 [85: 94: 102: 113] sts.

Change to 3¼mm (US 3) needles.

Row 30 (WS): Using yarn A, purl.

Beg and ending rows as indicated, cont in patt from chart for lower section as folls:

Work 46 rows, ending with RS facing for next row.

Place pocket

Next row (RS): Patt 10 [12: 14: 17: 20] sts, slip next 43 [43: 45: 45: 47] sts onto a holder (for pocket top) and, in their place, patt across 43 [43: 45: 45: 47] sts of first pocket lining, patt 25 [30: 35: 40: 46] sts.

Cont straight until 32 [32: 36: 36: 38] rows less have been worked than on back to beg of yoke patt, ending with RS facing for next row.

Shape front slope

Keeping patt correct, dec 1 st at end of next and foll 14 [14: 16: 16: 17] alt rows. 63 [70: 77: 85: 95] sts.

Work 1 row, ending with RS facing for next row.

Next row (RS): Using yarn A K7 [7: 8: 7: 5], M1, (K16 [14: 15: 14: 14], M1) 3 [4: 4: 5: 6] times, K8 [7: 9: 8: 6]. 67 [75: 82: 91: 102] sts.

Break off yarn A and complete left front using yarn B **only**.

Next row (WS): Purl.

Beg and ending rows as indicated, cont in patt from chart for yoke as folls:

Keeping patt correct, dec 1 st at end of next and foll 3 [5: 1: 1: 3] alt rows, then on 7 [6: 8: 8: 7] foll 4th rows. 56 [63: 72: 81: 91] sts.

Cont straight until left front matches back to beg of shoulder shaping, ending with RS facing for next row.

Shape shoulder

Keeping patt correct, cast off 9 [10: 12: 13: 15] sts at beg of next and foll 3 [2: 4: 2: 4] alt rows, then 10 [11: -: 14: -] sts at beg of foll 1 [2: -: 2: -] alt rows.

Work 1 row.

Cast off rem 10 [11: 12: 14: 16] sts.

RIGHT FRONT

Using 2¾mm (US 2) needles and yarn A cast on 78 [84: 94: 102: 112] sts.

Row 1 (RS): K2, *P1, K1, rep from * to end.

Row 2: *P1, K1, rep from * to end.

These 2 rows form rib.

Work in rib for a further 27 rows, inc 0 [1: 0: 0: 1] st at end of last row and ending with **WS** facing for next row. 78 [85: 94: 102: 113] sts.

Change to 3¼mm (US 3) needles.

Row 30 (WS): Using yarn A, purl.

Beg and ending rows as indicated, cont in patt from chart for lower section as folls:

Work 46 rows, ending with RS facing for next row.

Place pocket

Next row (RS): Patt 25 [30: 35: 40: 46] sts, slip next 43 [43: 45: 45: 47] sts onto a holder (for pocket top) and, in their place, patt across 43 [43: 45: 45: 47] sts of second pocket lining, patt 10 [12: 14: 17: 20] sts.

Complete to match first side, reversing shapings.

SLEEVES

Using 2¾mm (US 2) needles and yarn A cast on 55 [59: 61: 61: 63] sts.

Work in rib as given for back for 29 rows, ending with **WS** facing for next row.

Change to 3¼mm (US 3) needles.

Row 30 (WS): Using yarn A, purl.

Beg and ending rows as indicated, cont in patt from chart for lower section as folls:

Inc 1 st at each end of next and every foll alt row to 83 [87: 91: 103: 113] sts, then on every foll 4th row until there are 111 [117: 121: 127: 133] sts, taking inc sts into patt.

Work 1 row, ending with RS facing for next row.

Next row (RS): Using yarn A K7 [6: 8: 7: 6], M1, (K16 [13: 13: 14: 15], M1) 6 [8: 8: 8: 8] times, K8 [7: 9: 8: 7]. 118 [126: 130: 136: 142] sts.

Break off yarn A and complete sleeve using yarn B **only**.

Next row (WS): Purl.

Beg and ending rows as indicated, cont in patt from chart for yoke as folls:

Cont straight until sleeve meas 42 [43: 44: 44: 44] cm, ending with RS facing for next row.

Cast off.

YOKE CHART

KEY

☐ K on RS, P on WS   • P on RS, K on WS   ▨ Tw2R   ◩ Tw2L

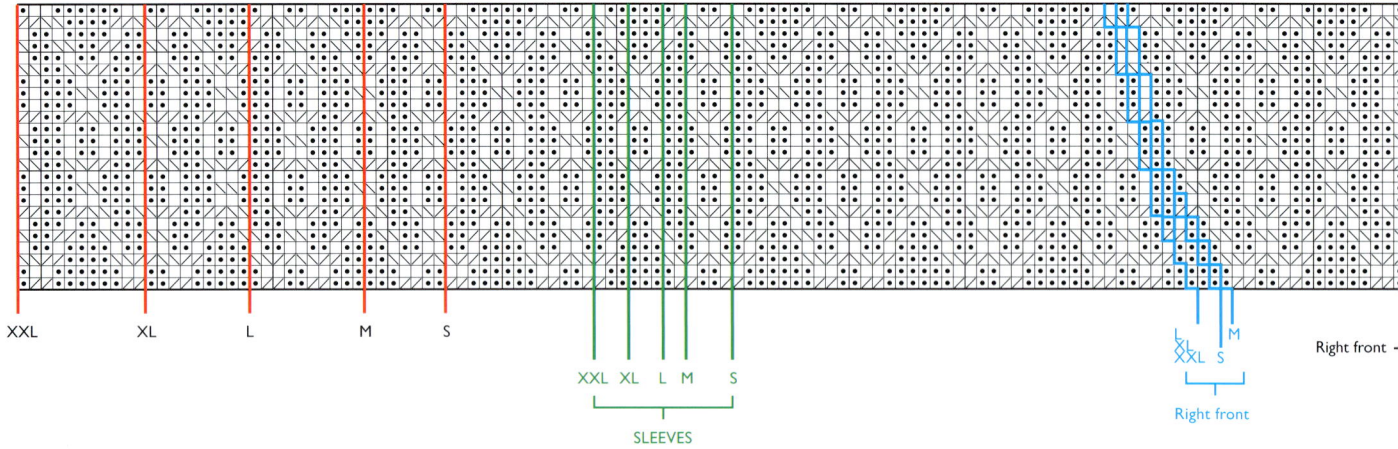

XXL   XL   L   M   S

XXL   XL   L   M   S

SLEEVES

L
XL
XXL   M
S

Right front

Right front

LOWER SECTION CHART

KEY

A. ☐ Clay 177   B. ✕ Granite 191

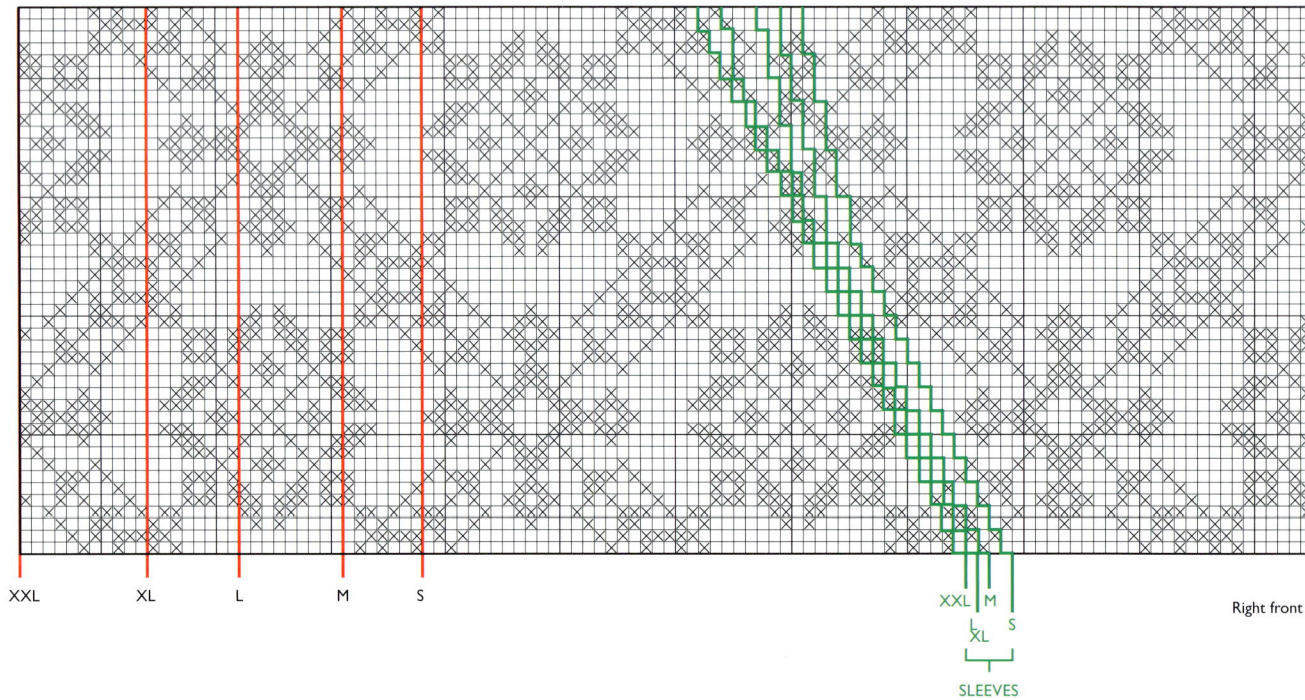

XXL   XL   L   M   S

Right front

XXL   M
L XL   S

SLEEVES

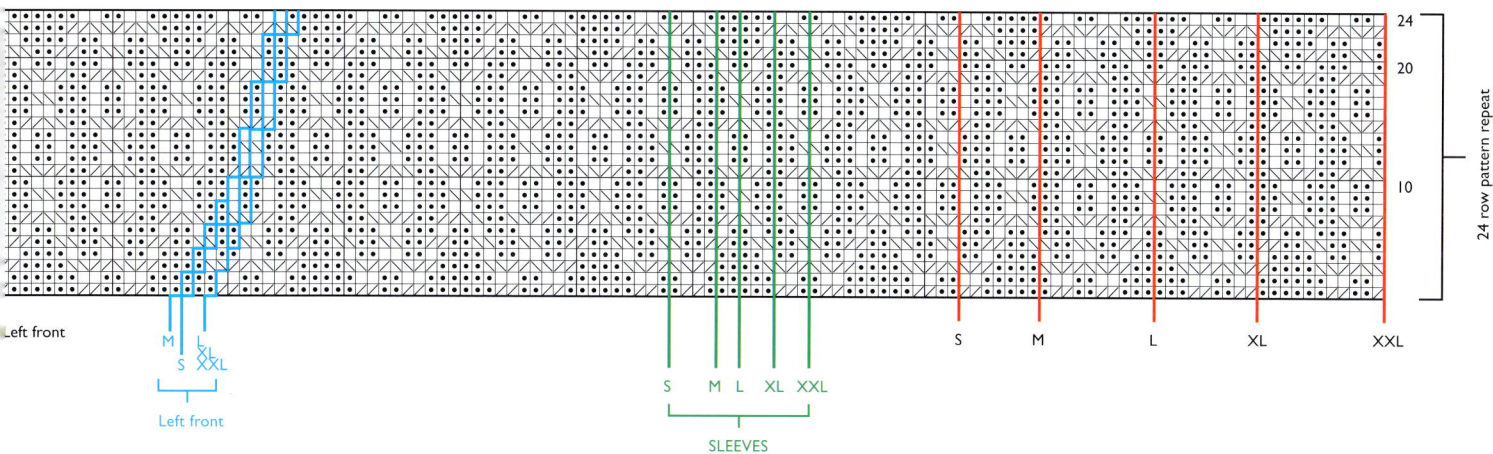

Left front

M L
S XL
   XXL

Left front

S M L XL XXL

SLEEVES

S   M   L   XL   XXL

24 row pattern repeat

24
20
10

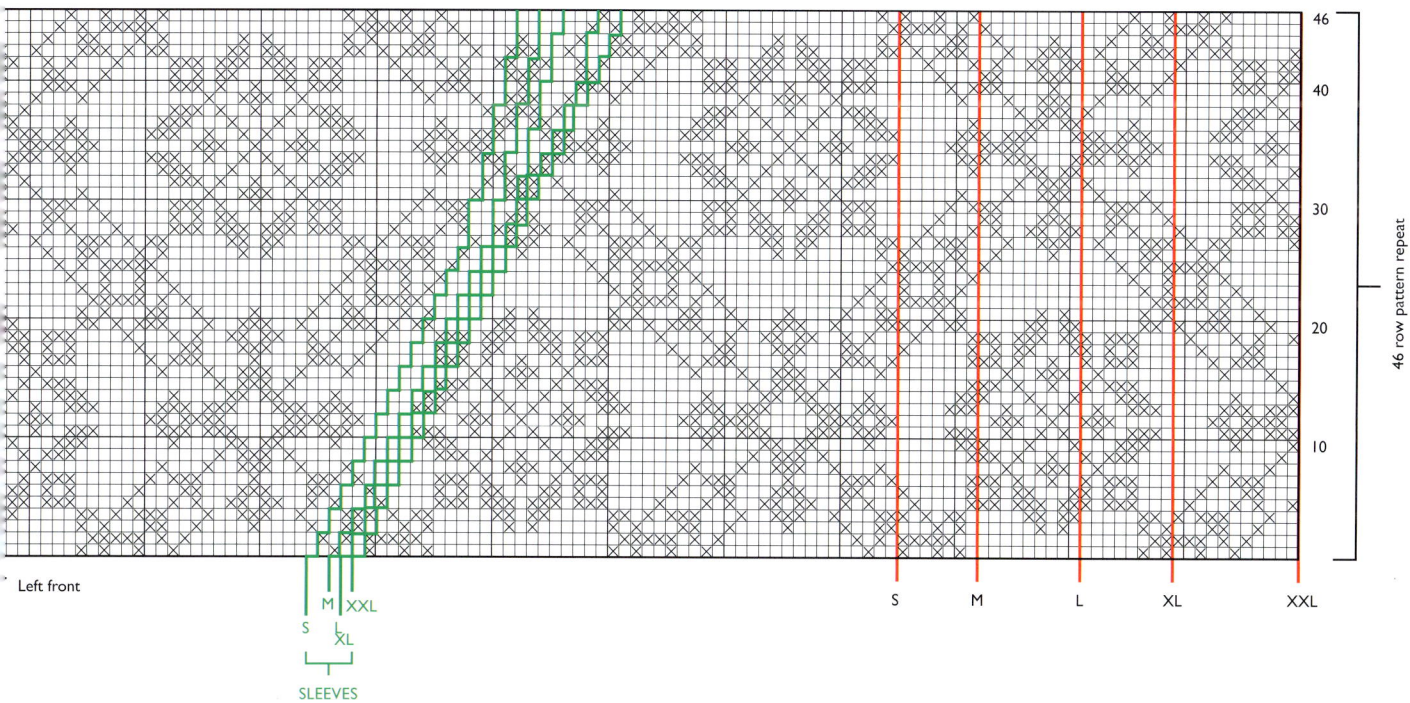

Left front

M XXL
S XL

SLEEVES

S   M   L   XL   XXL

46 row pattern repeat

46
40
30
20
10

MAKING UP

Press as described on the information page.

Join both shoulder seams using back stitch, or mattress stitch if preferred.

Front band

With RS facing, using 2¾mm (US 2) circular needle and yarn A, beg and ending at front cast-on edges, pick up and knit 122 [128: 134: 140: 146] sts evenly up right front opening edge to beg of front slope shaping, 81 [81: 84: 84: 87] sts up right front slope, and 5 sts down right side of back neck, K across 48 [48: 50: 50: 52] sts on back holder dec 3 sts evenly, then pick up and knit 5 sts up left side of back neck, 81 [81: 84: 84: 87] sts down left front slope to beg of front slope shaping, and 122 [128: 134: 140: 146] sts evenly down left front opening edge. 461 [473: 493: 505: 525] sts.

Row 1 (WS): K1, *P1, K1, rep from * to end.

Row 2: K2, *P1, K1, rep from * to last st, K1.

These 2 rows form rib.

Work in rib for 1 row more, ending with RS facing for next row.

Row 4 (RS): Rib 5, *yrn, work 2 tog (to make a buttonhole), rib 17 [18: 19: 20: 21], rep from * 5 times more, yrn, work 2 tog (to make 7th buttonhole), rib to end.

Work in rib for a further 3 rows, ending with RS facing for next row.

Cast off in rib.

Pocket tops (both alike)

Slip 43 [43: 45: 45: 47] sts on pocket holder onto 2¾mm (US 2) needles and rejoin yarn A with RS facing.

Next row (RS): Knit.

Beg with row 1, work in rib as given for front band for 7 rows, ending with RS facing for next row.

Cast off in rib.

Mark points along side seam edges 20 [21: 22: 23: 24] cm either side of shoulder seams and sew sleeves to back and fronts between these points. Join side and sleeve seams. Sew pocket linings in place on inside, then neatly sew down ends of pocket tops. Sew on buttons.

ISLAY

● ●

To fit bust	S	M	L	XL	XXL	
	81-86	91-97	102-107	112-117	122-127	cm
	32-34	36-38	40-42	44-46	48-50	in

Rowan Felted Tweed

		7	8	9	10	11	x 50gm

(photographed in Maritime 167)

Needles

1 pair 2¾mm (no 12) (US 2) needles
1 pair 3¼mm (no 10) (US 3) needles
Cable needle

Tension

27 sts and 36 rows to 10 cm measured over st st, 35 sts and 36 rows to 10 cm measured over patt, both using 3¼mm (US 3) needles.

SPECIAL ABBREVIATIONS

C4B = slip next 2 sts onto cable needle and leave at back of work, K2, then K2 from cable needle; **C4F** = slip next 2 sts onto cable needle and leave at front of work, K2, then K2 from cable needle; **C6B** = slip next 4 sts onto cable needle and leave at back of work, K2, slip centre 2 sts of

54 [56: 58: 60: 62] cm
(21½ [22: 23: 23½: 24½] in)

Width at underarm
44 [49: 55: 61: 68] cm
(17½ [19½: 21½: 24: 27] in)

44 [45: 46: 46: 46] cm
(17½ [17½: 18: 18: 18] in)

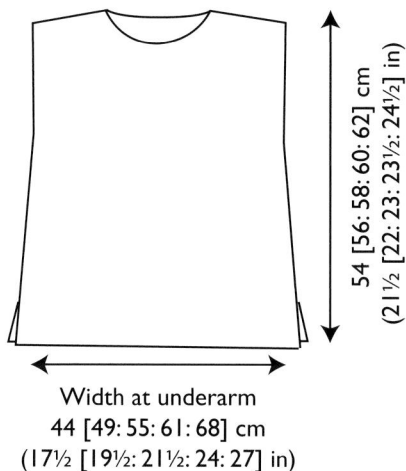

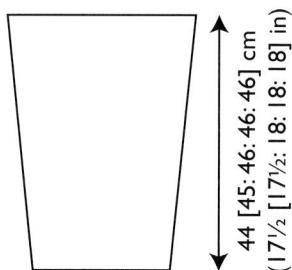

this group of 6 sts back onto left needle and P these 2 sts, then K2 from cable needle; **C6F** = slip next 4 sts onto cable needle and leave at front of work, K2, slip centre 2 sts of this group of 6 sts back onto left needle and P these 2 sts, then K2 from cable needle; **Cr4L** = slip next st onto cable needle and leave at front of work, K1, P2, then K1 from cable needle; **Cr4R** = slip next 3 sts onto cable needle and leave at back of work, K1, then P2, K1 across 3 sts on cable needle; **Tw2L** = K into back of second st on left needle, K tog tbl first 2 sts on left needle and slip both sts off left needle together; **Tw2R** = K2tog leaving sts on left needle, K first st again and slip both sts off left needle together.

BACK

Using 2¾mm (US 2) needles cast on 166 [182: 206: 226: 250] sts.
Row 1 (WS): (K1, P1) twice, K2, *P2, K2, rep from * to last 4 sts, (P1, K1) twice.
Row 2: K2, P1, K1, P2, *Tw2R, P2, rep from * to last 4 sts, K1, P1, K2.
These 2 rows form fancy rib.
Work in fancy rib for a further 18 rows, ending with **WS** facing for next row.

Row 21 (WS): Rib 10 [14: 10: 12: 12], work 2 tog, (rib 2, work 2 tog) 36 [38: 46: 50: 56] times, rib 10 [14: 10: 12: 12].
129 [143: 159: 175: 193] sts.
Place markers at both ends of last row (to denote top of side seam openings).
Change to 3¼mm (US 3) needles.
Beg with a K row, now work in st st as folls:
Dec 1 st at each end of 15th and 4 foll 14th rows.
119 [133: 149: 165: 183] sts.
Cont straight until back meas 32 [33: 34: 35: 36] cm, ending with **WS** facing for next row.
Next row (WS): P8 [9: 11: 10: 10], M1P, (P3, M1P) 34 [38: 42: 48: 54] times, P9 [10: 12: 11: 11]. 154 [172: 192: 214: 238] sts.
Beg and ending rows as indicated and repeating the 26 row patt repeat throughout, cont in patt from chart as folls:
Cont straight until back meas 51 [53: 55: 57: 59] cm, ending with RS facing for next row.

Shape shoulders and back neck

Keeping patt correct, cast off 7 [9: 10: 12: 14] sts at beg of next 2 rows.
140 [154: 172: 190: 210] sts.
Next row (RS): Cast off 7 [9: 10: 12: 14] sts, patt until there are 37 [42: 49: 56: 63] sts on right needle and turn, leaving rem sts on a holder.
Work each side of neck separately.
Dec 1 st at neck edge of next 6 rows **and at same time** cast off 7 [9: 10: 12: 14] sts at beg of 2nd and foll 0 [2: 0: 1: 2] alt rows, then 8 [-: 11: 13: -] sts at beg of foll 2 [-: 2: 1: -] alt rows.
Work 1 row.
Cast off rem 8 [9: 11: 13: 15] sts.
With RS facing, slip centre 52 [52: 54: 54: 56] sts onto a holder (for neckband), rejoin yarn and patt to end.
Complete to match first side, reversing shapings.

FRONT

Work as given for back until 12 [12: 16: 16: 20] rows less have been worked than on back to beg of shoulder shaping, ending with RS facing for next row.

Shape front neck

Next row (RS): Patt 56 [65: 75: 86: 98] sts and turn, leaving rem sts on a holder.
Work each side of neck separately.
Keeping patt correct, dec 1 st at neck edge of next 8 rows, then on foll 1 [1: 2: 2: 2] alt rows, then on 0 [0: 0: 0: 1] foll 4th row.
47 [56: 65: 76: 87] sts.
Work 1 [1: 3: 3: 3] rows, ending with RS facing for next row.

Shape shoulder

Cast off 7 [9: 10: 12: 14] sts at beg of next and foll 2 [4: 2: 3: 4] alt rows, then 8 [-: 11: 13: -] sts at beg of foll 2 [-: 2: 1: -] alt rows **and at same time** dec 1 st at neck edge of next and foll 4th row.
Work 1 row.
Cast off rem 8 [9: 11: 13: 15] sts.
With RS facing, slip centre 42 sts onto a holder (for neckband), rejoin yarn and patt to end.

□ K on RS, P on WS   • P on RS, K on WS   ⊠ Tw2L   ⬜ Tw2R   ⬜ C4F   ⬜ C4B   ⬜ C6B   ⬜ C6F   ⬜ Cr4L   ⬜ Cr4R

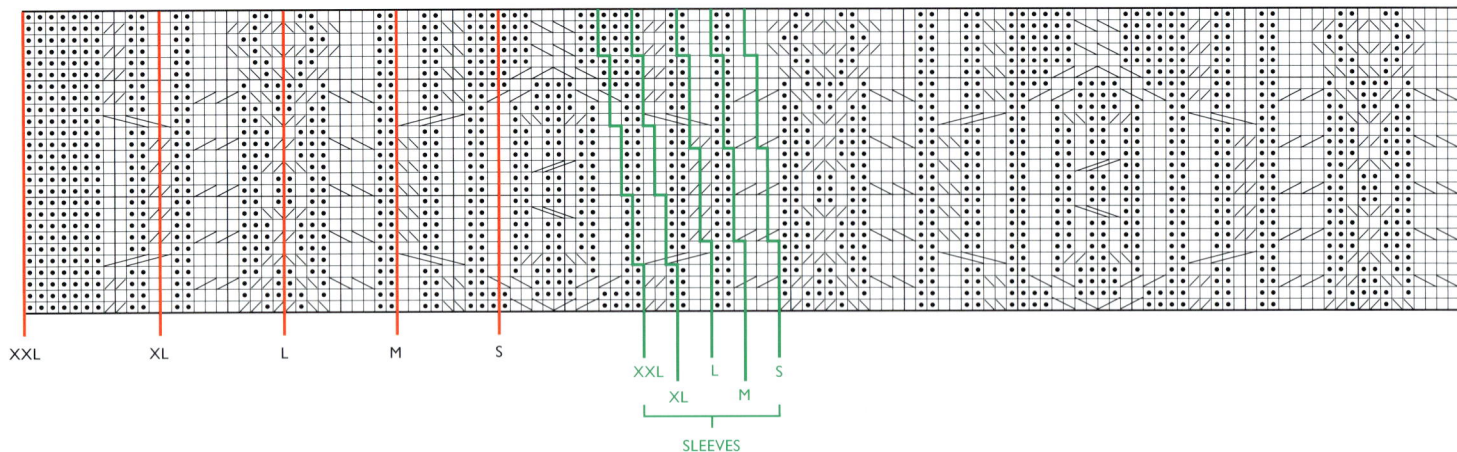

XXL   XL   L   M   S

XXL   L   S
XL   M

SLEEVES

Complete to match first side, reversing shapings.

SLEEVES
Using 2¾mm (US 2) needles cast on 62 [66: 66: 66: 70] sts.
Row 1 (WS): K2, *P2, K2, rep from * to end.
Row 2: P2, *Tw2R, P2, rep from * to end.
These 2 rows form fancy rib.
Work in fancy rib for a further 18 rows, ending with **WS** facing for next row.
Row 21 (WS): Rib 2 [2: 4: 4: 4], work 2 tog, (rib 5 [4: 5: 5: 4], work 2 tog) 8 [10: 8: 8: 10] times, rib 2 [2: 4: 4: 4]. 53 [55: 57: 57: 59] sts.
Change to 3¼mm (US 3) needles.
Beg with a K row, now work in st st as folls:
Inc 1 st at each end of 5th [5th: 5th: 3rd: 3rd] and every foll 6th [6th: 6th: 4th: 4th] row to 71 [77: 91: 69: 77] sts, then on every foll 8th [8th: -: 6th: 6th] row until there are 81 [85: -: 95: 99] sts, ending with **WS** facing for next row.
Next row (WS): P7 [6: 9: 8: 7], M1P, (P3, M1P) 22 [24: 24: 26: 28] times, P8 [7: 10: 9: 8]. 104 [110: 116: 122: 128] sts.
Beg and ending rows as indicated, cont in patt from chart as folls:
Inc 1 st at each end of 7th [7th: 7th: 5th: 5th] and every foll 8th [8th: 8th: 6th: 6th] row until there are 110 [116: 122: 130: 136] sts, taking inc sts into patt.
Cont straight until sleeve meas 44 [45: 46: 46: 46] cm, ending with RS

facing for next row.
Cast off.

MAKING UP
Press as described on the information page.
Join right shoulder seam using back stitch, or mattress stitch if preferred.
Neckband
With RS facing and using 2¾mm (US 2) needles, pick up and knit 19 [19: 21: 21: 23] sts down left side of front neck, K across 42 sts on front holder as folls: K2, (K2tog, K3) 8 times, pick up and knit 19 [19: 21: 21: 23] sts up right side of front neck, and 7 sts down right side of back neck, K across 52 [52: 54: 54: 56] sts on back holder as folls: K1 [1: 2: 2: 3], K2tog, (K4, K2tog) 8 times, K1 [1: 2: 2: 3], then pick up and knit 7 sts up left side of back neck. 129 [129: 135: 135: 141] sts.
Row 1 (WS): K1, *P1, K1, rep from * to end.
Row 2: P1, *K1, P1, rep from * to end.
These 2 rows form rib.
Cont in rib for a further 3 rows, ending with RS facing for next row.
Cast off in rib.
Join left shoulder and neckband seam. Mark points along side seam edges 17 [18: 19: 20: 21] cm either side of shoulder seams and sew sleeves to back and front between these points. Join side and sleeve seams, leaving side seams open below markers (for side seam openings).

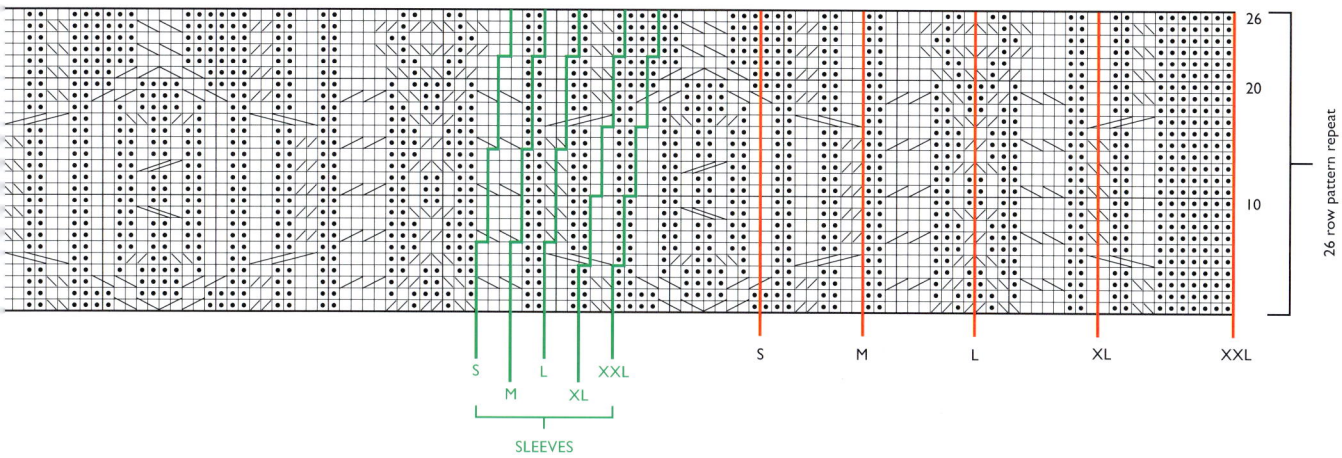

26

20

10

26 row pattern repeat

S

M

L

XL

XXL

SLEEVES

S

M

L

XL

XXL

TENSION

Achieving the correct tension is one of the most important factors when knitting one of my designs. I cannot stress highly enough that you really do need to knit a tension square BEFORE you start to knit the garment. The tension stated on each of my patterns must be achieved to ensure that the garment fits correctly and that it matches the measurements stated on the size diagram. I recommend that you knit a square using the number of stitches and rows stated on the pattern tension plus 3 or 4 stitches and rows. To check your tension, place the knitted square on a flat surface and mark out a 10cm square using pins as markers. Count the number of stitches and rows between the pins. If you have too many stitches, then your knitting is too tight, knit another square using a thicker needle. If you have too few stitches, then your knitting is too loose, knit another square using a thinner needle. It is also important to keep checking your tension whilst you are knitting your garment especially if you are returning to knit after leaving your work for a period of time.

SIZING

The patterns are written giving the instructions for the smallest size, for the other sizes work the figures in the brackets. The measurements stated on the size diagrams are the measurements of your finished garment AFTER pressing.

MODEL SIZE

Georgia is 5'8'' tall and is a standard size 8/10 and she is wearing the smallest size in each photograph.

STRANDED COLOUR WORK

Fair Isle is one of the main methods of adding colour into knitting. Fair Isle is used when mainly two are to be worked repeatedly along a row. The colour not being used is stranded fairly loosely behind the stitches being worked. It is very important not to pull this stranded yarn too tight as this will pucker your knitting and your stitch tension will be too tight, make sure to spread your stitches to ensure that they remain elastic. I would recommend that you carry the stranded or floating yarn over no more than 5 stitches when using a DK or 4 Ply yarn, and no more than 3 stitches when using an Aran or Chunky yarn. Weave the stranded colour under and over the colour being worked if you have to knit a colour over more than the recommended amount.

FINISHING

Finishing your garment beautifully is another important factor when making one of my designs. Good finishing will ensure that your garment fits correctly and washes and wears well. I urge you to spend time pressing and stitching your garment together, after all you've just spent a lot money and time knitting it using lovely Rowan yarns and the last thing you want to do is ruin it with bad finishing!

PRESSING

Firstly sew in any loose ends to the wrong side of the knitting. Block out each piece of knitting and then press according to the care instructions stated on the yarn ball bands. Always press using an iron on the wrong side of the knitting over a protective cloth (this can be damp or dry) and have the steam setting switched on the iron. Pay particular attention to the sides or edges of each piece as this will make the sewing up both easier and neater. Take special care with the welts and cuffs of the knitting – if the garment is fitted then gently steam the ribs so that they fill out but remain elastic. If the garment is a boxy, straight shape then steam press out the ribs to correct width.

STITCHING

When stitching the pieces together, remember to match areas of colour, texture or pattern very carefully where they meet. I recommend that you use mattress stitch wherever possible, this stitch gives the neatest finish ensuring that the seam lays flat.

Having knitted your pieces according to the pattern instructions, generally the shoulder seams of the front and back are now joined together using mattress stitch. Work the neck trim according to the pattern instructions and then join the neckband seams using mattress stitch if required. Knit neck bands or collars to the length stated in the pattern instructions, slightly stretching the trims before measuring if knitted in garter stitch or horizontal ribbing. Please take extra care when stitching the edgings and collars around the neck of the garment as these control the stretch of the neck. The sleeves are now normally added to the garment, take care to match the centre of the sleeve head to the shoulder seam. Ideally stretch the sleeve head into the armhole and stitch in place, if the sleeve head is too large for the armhole then check your tension as your knitting may be too loose. Join the underarm and side seams. Slip stitch any pockets or pocket lining into place and sew on buttons corresponding to the button holes lining up the outside edge of the button with the edging join or seam.

Carefully press your finished garment again to the measurements stated on the size diagram.

DIGITAL CHARTS

If you wish to receive a PDF copy of any of the charts within this collection then please send an email to: info@mariewallin.com with your request.

AFTERCARE

Ensure that you wash and dry your garment according to the care instructions stated on the yarn ball bands. If your garment uses more than one type of yarn then wash according to the most delicate. Reshape your garment when slightly damp and then carefully press to size again.

BUTTONS

The buttons used in this collection were kindly supplied by Textile Garden:

Textile Garden
1 Highland Croft
Steyning
BN44 3RF
UK
Tel: +44 (0) 1903 815759
        +44 (0) 7736 904109
Email: sales@textilegarden.com
Web: www.textilegarden.com

EXPERIENCE RATING

For guidance only.

● suitable for a beginner crocheter/knitter with a little experience.

● ● suitable for a crocheter/knitter with average ability.

● ● ● suitable for the experienced crocheter/knitter

KNITTING ABBREVIATIONS

K	knit
P	purl
st(s)	stitch(es)
inc	increas(e)(ing)
dec	decreas(e)(ing)
st st	stocking stitch (1 row K, 1 row P)
g st	garter stitch (K every row)
beg	begin(ning)
foll	ollowing
rem	remain(ing)
rev st st	reverse stocking stitch (1 row K, 1 row P)
rep	repeat
alt	alternate
cont	continue
patt	pattern
tog	together
mm	millimetres
cm	centimetres
in(s)	inch(es)
RS	right side
WS	wrong side
sl 1	slip one stitch
psso	pass slip stitch over
p2sso	pass 2 slipped stitches over
tbl	through back of loop
M1	make one stitch by picking up the horizontal loop before the next stitch and knitting into the back of it
M1P	make one stitch by picking up the horizontal loop before the next stitch and purling into the back of it
yfwd	yarn forward
yrn	yarn round needle
meas	measures
0	no stitches, times or rows
-	no stitches, times or rows for that size
yon	yarn over needle
yfrn	yarn forward round needle
wyib	with yarn at back